Ch...

Plain English

Boye Lafayette De Mente

PASSPORT BOOKS

NTC/Contemporary Publishing Company

Published by Passport Books
An imprint of NTC/Contemporary Publishing Company
4255 West Touhy Avenue, Lincolnwood (Chicago), Illinois 60646-1975 U.S.A.
Copyright © 1995 by Boye Lafayette De Mente
Printed in the United States of America
International Standard Book Number: 0-8442-8481-5
Library of Congress Catalog Card Number: 95-67178

20   19   18   17   16   15   14   13   12   11   10   9   8   7   6   5

Contents

Part Two   Communicating in Chinese   49–234

Part Three   General Vocabulary   235–332

Preface

It is common to speak of "Chinese" as if there were only one Chinese language. In a practical sense, however, there are at least seven Chinese languages, including Mandarin, Cantonese, Shanghainese, Hokkien, and Hunanese, along with dozens of Chinese dialects and minority-group languages.

While the Chinese languages and dialects belong to the same family—much like Spanish, Portuguese, Italian, and French are related—the seven primary languages are different enough that they are mutually unintelligible when spoken.

But all Chinese languages have traditionally been written with most of the same ideograms or "characters," so that speakers of Cantonese, Shanghainese, Hokkien, and so on are able to read each other's language fairly well, although their respective pronunciations are totally different.

Despite the generally common writing system, however, China's multiple languages have historically been a major divisive factor. The first serious attempt to create national standards for speaking, as well as writing, the various languages and dialects was made in 1913 by the Ministry of Education of the newly founded Chinese Republic. But conflicting regional interests, combined with ongoing political turmoil and wars, foiled these early attempts, which continued sporadically for several decades.

It was not until the Chinese Communist Party (CCP) came to power in 1949 and unified the country's administration that the necessary authority existed to undertake fundamental reform of the language problem. In 1956, the CCP decreed that the language spoken in the Beijing area and northern China, known to foreigners as Mandarin and in Mandarin as *Putonghua* or "Common Language," was to be the national language and thereafter would be taught in all schools throughout the country. At the same time, the CCP began steps to simplify and standardize the characters used to write Mandarin as well as the other Chinese languages.

By the mid-1990s, virtually all Chinese born after 1970, regardless of their native tongue, could understand and speak *Putonghua* fairly well, and many had become bilingual. Mandarin is now listed as the primary language in over 70 percent of the country. Mandarin is also taught and widely used in Taiwan and Singapore. Younger generations in these areas generally speak both Mandarin and their local dialect or language. Today, Mandarin Chinese is spoken by more people than any other language. English is second in number of speakers, Hindi is third, and Spanish is fourth. More than half of the population of the earth speaks one or the other of these four languages.

Part of the reputation that Chinese languages have traditionally had for being difficult to learn derives from the formidable nature and complexity of their pictographic writing system. Another facet of this reputation comes from the tonal characteristics of the languages. These two factors produce a mental barrier that makes many people shy away from studying any of the Chinese languages. It is also worth noting that until modern times, it was a felony crime for a native of China to teach Chinese to a foreigner and for foreigners to learn any of the languages.

Chinese in Plain English is designed to help break down any residual emotional barriers to learning Chinese and make it possible for you to immediately begin communicating in Chinese on a basic level. Every Chinese word and phrase in the book is phoneticized in "plain English." All you have to do to begin "speaking" Chinese is to enunciate the English phonetics.

Most people use fewer than 1,000 words of their native language in their daily lives. Communicating effectively is not so much how many words you know but what those words are and how they are used. This is particularly true in the case of basic communication in a second language. With a vocabulary of only a few hundred Chinese words, even if used one word at a time, you can communicate over 1,000 ideas—enough to help you survive while traveling or working in China and to enjoy yourself as well.

To avoid confusion, all subsequent references to the "Chinese language" in this book refer to Mandarin Chinese.

Boye Lafayette De Mentc

PART ONE

Breaking the Language Barrier

Some Facts about Chinese

Chinese is made up of 405 basic syllables, many of which have different tonal pronunciations, for a total of some 1,277 "building blocks." At first glance, this large number of syllables and building blocks makes Chinese appear extraordinarily complex. By comparison, the English language has only 44 basic sounds. But those 44 sounds are used to make up *several thousand* syllables, and, in that sense, English is far more complicated than Chinese.

The Chinese syllabic alphabet is made up of combinations of 5 vowel sounds, 15 compound vowels (combinations of the five basic sounds), and 23 consonants (21 if you discount "y" and "w," which the Chinese consider variations of "i" and "u"). These are combined in sound patterns that are repeated over and over, making the learning and pronunciation of the 405 syllables much less formidable than they might first appear. To make this challenge even less intimidating in both appearance and reality, I have included a phoneticized pronunciation guide that lists all of the Chinese syllables in a format that shows their phonetic relationship to each other.

Grammatically, Chinese is easier than English. The sentence order is generally subject, verb, object, just as it is in English; and adjectives come before nouns, just as they do in English. But, in Chinese, there are no plurals, no articles (the, a, or an), and no verb conjugations.

Other key features of Chinese include the following:

1. The subject of sentences (I, he, she, they, it) is generally not expressed when it is obvious from the context.
2. In addition to the usual way of forming questions (using interrogative words and a questioning tone),

adding the special interrogative word *ma* (mah) at the end of a sentence turns it into a question.

3. Possession is shown by using the word *de* (duh) between the pronoun and noun.

4. A "measure word" is always used between the number and noun when referring to a number or quantity of people or things. There are different measure words for various types of people and things.

   There is one special measure word, *ge* (guh), that is more or less universal and can be used when referring to any category of people or things. Although it is not technically correct in all cases and would not be used universally by fluent speakers, it nevertheless makes the meaning clear and is acceptable if you don't know the proper term.

5. The Chinese language does not have precise words for "yes" and "no." Although there are terms that have similar meanings, the Chinese generally use the negative or positive of the appropriate verb or adjective to express these concepts. For example, in answering the question, *chi*? (are you going to eat?), the normal response is *chi*, which literally means "eat" and figuratively means, "Yes, I'm going to eat." *Bu chi* ("No eat" or "No, I'm not going to eat") is used in a negative reponse.

   Putting *bu* in front of verbs and adjective makes them negative, but *bu* is not used by itself. There is another negative indicator, *mei*, that has its own special uses.

   As mentioned above, Chinese verbs do not conjugate. *Chi* remains the same, whatever tense of the verb is intended.

   There are, however, modifiers (*le* and *guo*) that are added to sentences to indicate the past tense. *Le* indicates the immediate past and *guo* signifies the distant past.

Modifiers (*yao* and *jiang*) are also used to indicate the future tense. *Yao*, placed after the subject, means "will" or "want to." For example,

I go (or I am going)	*wo qu*	(waw chu)
I went	*wo qu le*	(waw chu luh)
I will go	*wo jiang qu*	(waw jee-ahng chu)

Chinese Pronunciation

The first Europeans to take up residence in China were frustrated by the complexity of the pictographic system used to write the various Chinese languages. Some of the more scholarly of these early visitors soon created phonetic systems for writing Chinese in their own roman letters. A romanization system developed by two Englishmen named Wade and Giles in the mid-1800s eventually became the most popular among English speakers because it most closely resembled familiar English sounds. But, shortly after the Chinese Communist Party took over China in 1949, its leaders decided to adopt a roman phonetic system based on the Mandarin pronunciation that was prevalent in the Beijing area.

This official Chinese system for romanizing Mandarin, which went into effect in 1958, is called *pinyin* or "phonetic transcription," which is short for *pinyin zimu* or "phonetic alphabet." In simple terms, *pinyin* means "spelling." Since the *pinyin* phonetics system was not devised specifically for English speakers, several of the roman letters used in the system are pronounced quite differently than they are in English. The most conspicuous of these "mispronounced" letters are *c*, *q*, *x*, *z*, and the combination *zh*. *C* is pronounced more or less as "*ts*," *q* as "*ch*," *x* as "*sh*," *z* as "*dz*," and *zh* as "*j*."

In some words in the system, *u* is pronounced more like *o* and *e* is pronounced more like *u*. Similarly, *b* often comes out sounding very much like *p*; *d* may sound like *t*; and *g* may sound like *k*. The rest of the consonants (*f*, *h*, *j*, *k*, *l*, *m*, *n*, *p*, *s*, *t*, *w*, and *y*) are pronounced more or less as they are in English.

Another disconcerting factor is that the Chinese themselves disagree on the "correct" pronunciation of many syllables and words, often depending on which region they come from, as well as their age and educational level. This factor is especially noticeable when trying to render Chinese into English phonetics that are acceptable to everyone.

With the help of young native Mandarin speakers, this book makes a number of adaptions to the Wade-Giles system to make it easier for English speakers to pronounce Mandarin as if it were plain English. A number of common English words are used in place of phonetics when their pronunciation is exactly the same or nearly the same as the Chinese syllable concerned. For example, *hai* is pronounced "high," and *zhou* is "joe."

The 405 Chinese syllables are divided into five "sets" based on the key vowel sound in their pronunciation. The first set, consisting of some 100 syllables, is made up of the vowel sound *a* (ah) combined with ordinary consonants (*b*, *c*, *d*, *f*, *g*, and so on). The second set, which also consists of about 100 syllables, is based on the two vowel sounds *i* (ee) and *e* (eh) combined with several consonants. The third set of syllables is based on the *i* (ee) vowel. The fourth set of syllables is based on the *o* (oh) vowel and the last set is based on the *u* (uu) vowel.

The primary fear about pronouncing Chinese is not the number of syllables, but the infamous sing-song tones with which many of them must be pronounced to make the meaning clear. The meanings of a significant percentage of all Chinese words are determined by these tones. In addition, there are an especially large number of Chinese words that are pronounced exactly the same but have different meanings. Fortunately, Mandarin Chinese, the national language, has only four tones and is therefore the easiest of the Chinese languages to learn.

The Chinese tones are not directly related to musical pitches, so you don't have to worry about being able to carry a tune. The key is to make sure that the four tones are recognizably different in pitch. The four Mandarin tones are described as *even* (which is generally spoken in a slightly higher than normal voice), *rising* (the voice goes from a normal to a higher pitch), *falling-rising* (the voice goes down and up), and *falling* (the voice goes from a high to a lower tone). These tones are indicated in the *pinyin* phonetic system by diacritical marks over the syllables. The even tone is indicated by a horizontal line; the rising tone is shown by a line sloping up; the falling-rising tone is represented by a u-shaped mark; and the falling tone is shown by a mark slanting downward. When there are no marks over the words, there are no tones. The words are pronounced "flat."

Although tones do, in fact, totally change the meanings of many words, a great deal of the meaning of any Chinese word or sentence is indicated by the context in which it is used, so there is some leeway in getting the pitches right. Furthermore, the Chinese have had eons of experience in dealing with other Chinese who speak their particular language or dialect poorly, and they are both lenient and helpful in communicating with each other and with foreigners.

The English phonetic system in this book is based on getting as close as possible to the correct Chinese pronunciation, without any attempt to account for tonal inflections. If you read the phonetics out loud or repeat them aloud as plain English, the sounds will either be right on or close enough to the correct Chinese pronunciation that you will be understood most of the time. Of course, if you have had phonetic training and want to use the *pinyin* spelling system with its diacritical marks as your pronunciation guide, so much the better.

In any event, communicating in Chinese must begin with the basic pronunciation of individual words. Learning to voice them in the right tone is the second step. Note that there is a constantly repeated sound pattern, both horizontally and vertically, in each of the syllable sets. All of the horizontal sound patterns are based on just five vowel sounds. The vertical patterns are based on the familiar consonants plus the vowel sounds. You should drill yourself on these pronunciation charts until you can enunciate each syllable easily and smoothly, without having to think about it. Before long, you will be able to recognize individual syllables in the Chinese words you see and hear.

When the Chinese write their language they generally do not separate the "words" with spaces. The characters making up the words are run together as solid blocks of type. This practice has been carried over into the transliteration of Chinese words into roman letters. For example, Beijing's famous square, *Tiananmen*, is written as one word. But it consists of three pictographic compounds, *Tian An Men* (Tee-ahn Ahn Mun), each of which is a separate word, literally "Heaven Peace Gate," or translated as "Gate of Heavenly Peace."

In some cases, Chinese "spellings" have been separated in the English fashion to make it easier to identify and pronounce the individual words.

Pronunciation Guide # 1

A	AI	AN	ANG	AO
ah	eye	ahn	ahng	ow
				(as in ouch)
BA	BAI	BAN	BANG	BAO
bah	buy	bahn	bahng	bow
CA	CAI	CAN	CANG	CAO
tsah	tsigh	tsahn	tsahng	tsow
CHA	CHAI	CHAN	CHANG	CHAO
chah	chigh	chahn	chahng	chow
DA	DAI	DAN	DANG	DAO
dah	die	dahn	dahng	dow
FA		FAN	FANG	
fah		fahn	fahng	
GA	GAI	GAN	GANG	GAO
gah	guy	gahn	gahng	gow
HA	HAI	HAN	HANG	HAO
hah	high	hahn	hahng	how
KA	KAI	KAN	KANG	KAO
kah	kigh	kahn	kahng	kow
				(as in cow)
LA	LAI	LAN	LANG	LAO
lah	lie	lahn	lahng	lou
				(as in loud)

MA mah	MAI my	MAN mahn	MANG mahng	MAO mou (as in mouth)
NA nah	NAI nigh	NAN nahn	NANG nahng	NAO now
PA pah	PAI pie	PAN pahn	PANG pahng	PAO pow
		RAN rahn	RANG rahng	RAO rou (as in rowdy)
SA sah	SAI sigh	SAN sahn	SANG sahng	SAO sow (as in pig)
SHA shah	SHAI shy	SHAN shahn	SHANG shahng	SHAO shou (as in shout)
TA tah	TAI tie	TAN tahn	TANG tahng	TAO tou (as in tout)
WA wah	WAI wigh	WAN wahn	WANG wahng	
YA yah			YANG yahng	YAO yow
ZA zah	ZAI zigh	ZAN zahn	ZANG zahng	ZAO zow

(Continued)

9

ZHA	ZHAI	ZHAN	ZHANG	ZHAO
jah	jigh	jahn	jahng	jow

Pronunciation Guide # 2

E	EI	EN	ENG	ER
uh	a*	un**	ung	ur
	BEI	BEN	BENG	
	bay	bin	buung	
CE		CEN	CENG	
tsuh		tswun	tsuung	
CHE		CHEN	CHENG	
chuh		chun	chuung	
DE			DENG	
duh			duung	
	FEI	FEN	FENG	
	fay	fin	fuung	
GE	GEI	GEN	GENG	
guh	gay	gun	guung	
HE	HEI	HEN	HENG	
huh	hay	hin	huung	
KE		KEN	KENG	
kuh		kin	kuung	

---

* EI is pronounced like the "ei" in eight.

** EN is pronounced as the "un" in pun or as the "in" in pin, depending on the word.

LE	LEI		LENG
luh	lay		luung
ME	MEI	MEN	MENG
muh	may	mun	muung
NE	NEI	NEN	NENG
nuh	nay	nun	nuung
	PEI	PEN	PENG
	pay	pin	puung
RE		REN	RENG
ruh		wren	ruung
SE		SEN	SENG
suh		sin	suung
SHE	SHEI	SHEN	SHENG
shuh	shay	shuun	shuung
TE			TENG
tuh			tuung
	WEI	WEN	WENG
	way	wun	wuung
YE			
yeh			
ZE	ZEI	ZEN	ZENG
zuh	zay	zen	zuung
ZHE	ZHEI	ZHEN	ZHENG
juh	jay	jun	juung

Pronunciation Guide # 3

BI	BIAN	BIAO	BIE	BIN	BING	
bee	bee-in*	bee-ow	bee-eh	bin	beeng	

| CHI | | | | | | |
| chee | | | | | | |

| CI | | | | | | |
| tsu | | | | | | |

| DI | DIAN | DIAO | DIE | | DING | DIU |
| dee | dee-in | dee-ow | dee-eh | | deeng | dew/deo |

| JI | JIAN | JIAO | JIE | JIN | JING | JIU |
| jee | jee-in | jee-ow | jee-eh | jeen | jeeng | jew/jeo |

| JIA | JIONG | | | | | |
| jee-ah | jee-ohng | | | | | |

| JIANG | | | | | | |
| jee-ahng | | | | | | |

---

* Phonetic terms divided by hyphens, like *bian* (bee-in), should be pronounced smoothly as one word.

	LIA / lee-ah	LIAN / lee-in	LIAO / lee-ow	LIE / lee-eh	LIN / leen	LING / leeng	LIU / lew/leo
LI lee	lee-ah	lee-in	lee-ow	lee-eh	leen	leeng	lew/leo
LIANG lee-ahng							
MI me		MIAN mee-in	MIAO mee-ow	MIE me-eh	MIN meen	MING meeng	MIU meo
NI nee		NIAN nee-in	NIAO nee-ow	NIE nee-eh	NIN neen	NING neeng	NIU neo
NIANG nee-ahng							
PI pee		PIAN pee-in	PIAO pee-ow	PIE pee-eh	PIN peen	PING peeng	

(Continued)

Pronunciation Guide # 3 (Continued)

QI chee	QIA chee-ah	QIAN chee-in	QIAO chee-ow	QIE chee-eh	QIN cheen	QING cheeng	QIU cheo
QIANG chee-ahng							
RI rr							
SHI shr							
SI suh							
TI tee		TIAN tee-in	TIAO tee-ow	TIE tee-eh		TING teeng	

XI	XIA	XIAN	XIAO	XIE	XIN	XING
she	shee-ah	shee-in	shee-ow	she-eh	sheen	sheeng
				XIU	XIANG	XIONG
				sheo	shee-ahng	shee-ong

YI					YIN	YING
ee					een	eeng

ZHI	ZI
jr	dzu

Pronunciation Guide # 4

BO
bwo/bwough

CHONG	CHOU	CONG	COU
choong	choe	tsoong	tsoe
		DONG	DOU
		doong	doe
FO			FOU
fwo/fwough			foe
		GONG	GOU
		goong	go
		HONG	HOU
		hoong	hoe
		KONG	KOU
		koong	koe
		LONG	LOU
		loong	low
MO			MOU
mwo/mwough			moe
		NONG	NOU
		noong	no
O			OU
aw			oh

PO			POU
pwaw			poe
		RONG	ROU
		roong	roe
	SHOU	SONG	SOU
	show	soong	soe
		TONG	TOU
		toong	toe
WO			
waw			
YO		YONG	YOU
yaw		yoong	yoe
ZHONG	ZHOU	ZONG	ZOU
joong	joe	zoong	zoe

Pronunciation Guide # 5

	-ua	-uai	-uan	-uang	-ui	-un	-uo
BU buu							
CHU chuu	CHUA chwah	CHUAI chwie	CHUAN chwahn	CHUANG chwahng	CHUI chwee chway	CHUN chwun	CHUO chwaw
CU tsu			CUAN tswahn		CUI tsway tswee	CUN tswun	CUO tswaw
DU duu			DUAN dwahn		DUI dway dwee	DUN dwun	DUO dwaw
FU fuu							

	GUA gwah	GUAI gwie	GUAN gwahn	GUANG gwahng	GUI gway gwee	GUN gwun	GUO gwaw
GU guu	GUA gwah	GUAI gwie	GUAN gwahn	GUANG gwahng	GUI gway gwee	GUN gwun	GUO gwaw
HU huu	HUA hwah	HUAI hwie	HUAN hwahn	HUANG hwahng	HUI hway hwee	HUN hwun	HUO hwaw
JU juu			JUAN jwen		JUE ju-eh	JUN jwin	
KU kuu	KUA kwah	KUAI kwie	KUAN kwahn	KUANG kwahng	KUI kway kwee	KUN kwun	KUO kwaw
LU luu			LUAN lwahn		LUE lu-eh	LUN lwun	LUO lwaw
MU muu							

(Continued)

Pronunciation Guide # 5 (Continued)

NU nuu			NUAN nwahn		NUE nu-eh		NUO nwaw
PU puu							
QU chu			QUAN chwahn			QUN chwun	
RU ruu			RUAN rwahn		RUI rway rwee	RUN rwun	RUO rwaw
SHU shuu	SHUA shwah	SHUAI shwie	SHUAN shwahn	SHUANG shwahng	SHUI shway shwee	SHUN shwun	SHUO shwaw
SU suu			SUAN swahn		SUI sway	SUN suun	SUO swaw

TU tuu			TUAN twahn		TUI tway	TUN twun	TUO twaw
WU wuu							
XU shu			XUAN shwen		XUE shu-eh	XUN shwun	
YU yuu			YUAN ywen		YUE yu-eh	YUN ywun	
ZHU juu	ZHUA jwah	ZHUAI jwie	ZHUAN jwahn	ZHUANG jwahng	ZHUI jway jwee	ZHUN juwun	ZHUO jwaw
ZU zuu			ZUAN zwahn		ZUI zway zwee	ZUN zwun	ZUO zwaw

Making Yourself at Home in China

The communication barrier most people face in their first contact with China begins with what the Chinese people call themselves and their country in their own language, which is about as basic as you get. When this communication block includes the names of the provinces, the cities (except perhaps for Beijing and Shanghai), and such famous landmarks as the Great Wall, one can imagine how significant the problem can be. Just *how* helpless a person can be in such a situation really comes home to newly arrived visitors when they discover that they are unable to correctly pronounce the name of the hotel where they are staying or the street it is on, and cannot come and go without a guide or a hotel identification card written in Chinese characters to show to taxi drivers and others.

Learning how to pronounce individual words is, of course, not the same as learning how to speak Chinese, but it is still a key part of becoming "fluent" in daily life in the country and the starting point for any language learning. By familiarizing yourself with the pronunciation of the following place names and key terms, you can greatly increase your ability to function effectively in China.

Even if you achieve only a modest degree of fluency in saying the words, it will help you feel much more at ease in talking about and actually dealing with China. Keep in mind that although the phonetic spellings are divided by hyphens, they should be pronounced as single words.

The Chinese Connection

China
Zhongguo
(Joong-gwaw)

People's Republic of China
Zhonghua Renmin Gongheguo
(Joong-hwah Wren-meen Goong-huh-gwaw)

Chinese (person)
Zhongguoren
(Joong-gwaw-wren)

Chinese (language)
Hanyu/Zhongwen*
(Hahn-yuu/Joong-wun)

Overseas Chinese
Hua Qiao
(Hwah Chee-ow)

Chinese-American
Meiji Huaren
(May-jee Hwah-wren)

Chinese-British
Yingji Huaren
(Eeng-jee Hwah-wren)

Beijinger
Beijingren
(Bay-jeeng-wren)

Cantonese
Guangdongren
(Gwahn-doong-wren)

---

* *Hanyu* is the "literary" term for Chinese. *Zhongwen* is the term generally used in ordinary speech.

Hong Kong/Hong Kongnese
Xiang Guang/Xiang Guangren
(She-ahng Gwahng/She-ahng Gwahng-wren)

Kowloon
Jiulong
(Jeo-loong)

Macao/Macaonese
Aomen/Aomenren
(Ow-mun/Ow-mun-wren)

Shanghainese
Shanghairen
(Shahng-high-wren)

Singapore/Singaporean
Xinjiapo/Xinjiaporen
(Sheen-jee-ah-pwaw/Sheen-jee-ah-pwaw-wren)

Taiwanese
Taiwanren
(Tie-wahn-wren)

China International Travel Service (CITS)
Guoji Luxing She
(Gwaw-jee Luu-sheeng Shuh)

Civil Aviation Administration of China (CAAC)
Zhongguo Min Hang
(Joong-gwaw Meen Hahng)

24

Foreign Nationalities

American	*Meiguoren*	(May-gwaw-wren)
Argentinian	*Arguntingren*	(Arh-gwun-teeng-wren)
Australian	*Aodaliyaren*	(Ah-aw-dah-lee-yah-wren)
Austrian	*Aodiliren*	(Ah-aw-dee-lee-wren)
Belgian	*Bilishiren*	(Bee-lee-shr-wren)
Brazilian	*Baxiren*	(Bah-she-wren)
British/ English	*Yinguoren*	(Een-gwaw-wren)
Canadian	*Jianadaren*	(Jeeah-nah-dah-wren)
Cuban	*Gubaren*	(Guu-bah-wren)
Danish	*Danmairen*	(Dahn-my-wren)
Dutch	*Helanren*	(Huh-lahn-wren)
Filipino	*Feilubinren*	(Fay-luu-bin-wren)
French	*Faguoren*	(Fah-gwaw-wren)
German	*Deguoren*	(Duh-gwaw-wren)

Greek	*Xilaren*	(She-lah-wren)
Indian	*Yinduren*	(Een-duu-wren)
Indonesian	*Yindunixiyaren*	(Een-duu-nee-she-yah-wren)
Italian	*Yidaliren*	(Ee-dah-lee-wren)
Japanese	*Ribenren*	(Rr-bin-wren)
Korean	*Chaoxianren*	(Chow-shee-in-wren)
Malaysian	*Malaixiyaren*	(Mah-lie-she-yah-wren)
Mexican	*Moxigeren*	(Mwo-she-guu-wren)
Mongolian	*Mengguren*	(Muung-guu-wren)
Myanmar	*Miandianren*	(Me-ahn-dee-in-wren)
New Zealander	*Xin Xilanren*	(Sheen She-lahn-wren)
Norwegian	*Nuoweiren*	(Nwaw-way-wren)
Pakistani	*Bajisidanren*	(Bah-jee-suh-dahn-wren)

Portuguese	*Putaoyaren*	(Puu-tou-yah-wren)
Russian	*Eguowren*	(Uh-gwaw-wren)
Singaporean	*Xinjiaporen*	(Sheen-jee-ah-pwaw-wren)
Spanish	*Xibanyaren*	(She-bahn-yah-wren)
Swedish	*Ruidianren*	(Rway-dee-ahn-wren)
Swiss	*Ruishiren*	(Rway-shr-wren)
Thai	*Taiguoren*	(Tie-gwaw-wren)
Ukrainian	*Ukulanren*	(Yuu-kuu-lahn-wren)
Vietnamese	*Yuenanren*	(Yuu-uh-nahn-wren)
I am American	*Wo shi Meiguoren*	(Waw shr May-gwaw-wren)

China's Provinces

Anhui (Ahn-hway)

Fujian (Fuu-jee-ahn)

Gansu (Gahn-suu)

Guangdong (Gwahng-doong)

27

Guizhou (Gway-joe)

Hainan (High-nahn)

Hebei (Huh-bay)

Heilongjiang (Hay-loong-jee-ahng)

Henan (Huh-nahn)

Hubei (Huu-bay)

Hunan (Huu-nahn)

Jiangxi (Jee-ahng-she)

Jilin (Jee-leen)

Liaoning (Lee-ow-neeng)

Qinghai (Cheeng-high)

Shaanxi (Shah-ahn-she)

Shandong (Shahn-doong)

Shanxi (Shahn-she)

Sichuan (Suh-chwahn)

Yunnan (Ywun-nahn)

Zhejiang (Juh-jee-ahng)

Add *ren* (wren) to any of these provincial names to signify people from the area. For example, Hunannese is *Hunanren* (Huu-nahn-wren).

Autonomous Regions of China

Guangxi Zhuang	Guangxi Zhuangzu	(Gwahng-she Jwahng-zuu)
Inner Mongolia	Nei Menggu	(Nay Muung-guu)

Ningxia Huizu	Ningxia Huizu	(Neeng-shee-ah Hway-zuu)
Tibet	Xizang	(She-zahng)
Xinjiang Uyghur	Xinjiang Weiwuerzu	(Sheen-jee-ahng Way-wuu-urr-zuu)

Major Cities in China

Anshan (Ahn-shahn)

Anyang (Ahn-yahng)

Aomen (Ow-mun)
(Macau)

Baotou (Bow-toe)

Beidaihe (Bay-die-huh)

Beihai (Bay-high)

Beijing (Bay-jeeng)

Changchun (Chahng-chwun)

Changsha (Chahng-shah)

Chengde (Chuung-duh)

Chengdu (Chuung-duu)

Chongqing (Choong-cheeng)
(Chungking)

Dali (Dah-lee)

Dalian (Dah-lee-in)

Daqing (Dah-cheeng)

Dunhuang (Dwun-hwahng)

Foshan (Fwo-shahn)

Fuzhou (Fuu-joe)

Guangxi (Gwahng-she)

Guangzhou (Gwahng-joe)
(Canton)

Guiyang (Gway-yahng)

Hainan (High-nahn)

Harbin (Hah-urr-bin)

Hohhot (Huu-huh-how-tuh)
(Huheote)

Huang He (Hwahng Huh)

Jilin (Jee-leen)

Jinan (Jee-nahn)

Kaifeng (Kigh-fuung)

Kunming (Kwun-meeng)

Lanzhou (Lahn-joe)

Lhasa (Lah-sah)

Luda (Luu-dah)

Luoyang (Lwaw-yahng)

Lu Shan (Luu-Shahn)
(Lushun)

Nanchang (Nahn-chahng)

Nanjing (Nahn-jeeng)
(Nanking)

Nanning (Nahn-neeng)

Ninghho (Neeng-bwo)

Ningxia (Neeng-shee-ah)

Qingdao (Cheeng-dow)

Qinghai (Cheeng-high)

Qinhuangdao (Cheen-hwahng-dow)

Quanzhou (Chwen-joe)

Qufu (Chu-fuu)

Shanghai (Shahng-high)

Shanghaiguan (Shahng-high-gwahn)

Shantou (Shahn-toe)

Shaoshan (Shou-shahn)

Shenyang (Shuun-yahng)
(Mukden)

Shenzhen (Shuun-jun)

Shijiazhuang (Shr-jee-ah-jwahng)

Suzhou (Suu-joe)

Taiyuan (Tie-ywen)

Tianjin (Tee-in-jeen)

Turpan (Turr-pahn)

Urumqi (Uu-ruum-chee)

Wenzhou (Wun-joe)

Wuhan (Wuu-hahn)

Wutai Shan (Wuu-tie Shawn)

Wuxi (Wuu-she)

Xiamen (Shee-ah-mun)
(Amoy)

Xian/Sian (Shee-in)

Xiang Guang (Shee-ahng Gwahng)
(Hong Kong)

Xinjiang (Sheen-jee-ahng)

Yanan (Yah-nahn)

Yangzhou (Yahng-joe)

Yenan (Yeh-nahn)

Yixing (Ee-sheeng)

Zhenjiang (Jun-jee-ahng)

Zhengzhou (Juung-joe)

Zhuhai (Juu-high)

Beijing Landmarks

Baiyun (Daoist) Temple	Baiyun Guan	(Buy-ywun Gwahn)
Behai Park	Beihai Gongyuan	(Bay-high Goong-ywen)
Beijing University	Beijing Daxue	(Bay-jeeng Dah-shu-uh)
Beijing Zoo	Beijing Dongwuyuan	(Bay-jeeng Doong-wuu-ywen)
Coal Hill	Jing Shan	(Jeeng Shahn)
Forbidden City	Zijin Cheng	(Dzu-jeen Chuung)
Front Gate	Qian Men	(Chee-in Mun)

Gate of Supreme Harmony	Tai He Men	(Tie Huh Mun)
Great Hall of the People	Renmin Dahuitang	(Wren-meen Dah-hway-tahng)
Guguanxiangtai Observatory	Gu Guanxiang Tai	(Guu Gwahn-shee-ahng Tie)
Hall of Perfect Harmony	Zhong He Dian	(Joong Huh Dee-in)
Hall of Preserving Harmony	Bao He Dian	(Bow Huh Dee-in)
Hall of Supreme Harmony	Tai He Dian	(Tie Huh Dee-in)
Hall of Union	Jiao Tai Dian	(Jee-ow Tie Dee-in)
Imperial Gardens	Yuhuan Yuan	(Yuu-hwahn Ywen)
Imperial Palace	Gu Gong	(Guu Goong)
Mao Zedong Memorial Mausoleum	Mao Zedong Jinian Tang	(Mou Zuh-duung Jee-nee-in Tahng)

Marco Polo Bridge	Lugou Qiao	(Luu-gwaw Chee-ow)
Meridian Gate	Wu Men	(Wuu Mun)
Museum of Chinese History	Zhongguo Lishi Bowuguan	(Joong-gwaw Lee-shr Bwo-wuu-gwahn)
Museum of the Chinese Revolution	Zhongguo Gemin Bowuguan	(Joong-gwaw Guu-meen Bwo-wuu-gwahn)
National Library	Zhongguoguo Tushuguan	(Joong-gwaw-gwaw Tuu-shuu-gwahn)
Nationalities Cultural Palace	Minzu Wenhua Gong	(Meen-zuu Wun-hwah Goong)
North Lake Park	Beihai Gongyuan	(Bay-high Goong-ywen)
Palace of Earthly Tranquility	Kun Ning Gong	(Kwun Neeng Goong)
Palace of Heavenly Purity	Qian Qing Gong	(Chee-in Cheeng Goong)
Palace Temple	Yonghe Gong	(Yoong-huh Goong)

People's Cultural Park	Renmin Wenhua Gongyuan	(Wren-meen Wun-hwah Goong-ywen)
Summer Palace	Yihe Yuan	(Ee-huh Ywen)
Taoranting Park	Taoranting Gongyuan	(Tah-aw-rahn-teeng Goong-ywen)
Temple of Heaven	Tian Tan	(Tee-in Tahn)
Tiananmen Square	Tian An Men Guangchang	(Tee-in Ahn Mun Gwahng-chahng)
Xidan Market	Xidan Shichang	(She-dahn Shr-chahng)
Yuyuan Lake	Yuyuan Hu	(Yuu-ywen Huu)
Zhongshan Park	Zhongshan Gongyuan	(Joong-shahn Goong-ywen)

Beijing Vicinity

| Great Wall | Chang Cheng | (Chahng Chuung) |
| Ming Tombs | Shi San Ling | (Shr Sahn Leeng) |

Department Stores in Beijing

| Dongfeng Market | Dongfeng Shichang | (Doong-fuung Shr-chahng) |

Friendship Store	Youyi Shang Dian	(Yoe-ee Shahng Dee-in)
main department store	baihuo da lou	(buy-hwaw dah low)
Xidan Emporium	Xidan Baihuo Shangchang	(Shi-dahn Buy-hwaw Shahng-chahng)

Shopping Districts in Beijing

Jianguomenwai	Jian Guo Men Wai	(Jee-in Gwaw Mun Wigh)
Liulichang	Liu Li Chang	(Lee-oh Lee Chahng)
Qianmen	Qian Men	(Chee-in Mun)
Wangfujing	Wang Fu Jing	(Wahng Fuu Jeeng)
Xidan	Xi Dan	(She Dahn)

Beijing's Main Streets

Avenue/street	Dajie (Dah-jee-eh)
Avenue/street	Jie (Jee-eh)
Gate	Men (Mun)
Road/route	Lu (Luu)

Andingmen Road	(Ahn-deeng-mun Luu)
Baishiqiao Road	(Buy-shr-chee-ow Luu)
Baizhifang Street	(Buy-jr-fahng Jee-eh)
Beihuan Dong Road	(Bay-hwahn Doong Luu)
Beiyuan Road	(Bay-ywen Luu)
Changan Tujing Road	(Chahng-ahn Tuu-jeeng Luu)
Changping Road	(Chahng-peeng Luu)
Chaoyangmen Road	(Chow-yahng-mun Luu)
Dianmen Street	(Dee-in-mun Jee-eh)
Dongdan Street	(Doong-dahn Jee-eh)
Donghuan Bei Road	(Doong-hwahn Bay Luu)
Donghuan Nan Road	(Doong-hwahn Nahn Luu)
Dongsi Street	(Doong-suh Dah-jee-eh)
Dongzhimen Nei Road	(Doong-jr-mun Nay Luu)
Dongzhimen Wai Road	(Doong-jr-mun Wigh Luu)
Fucheng Road	(Fuu-chuung Luu)
Fuchengmen Road	(Fuu-chuung-mun Luu)
Fuxing Road	(Fuu-sheeng Luu)
Fuxingmen Avenue	(Fuu-sheeng-mun Jee-eh)
Gongren Tiyuchang Road	(Goong-wren Tee-yuu-chahng Luu)
Guanan Road	(Gwahn-ahn Luu)
Guananmen Avenue	(Gwahn-ahn-mun Jee-eh)
Haidian Road	(High-dee-in Luu)
Janhuachi Road	(Jahn-hwah-chee Luu)

Jianguomen Avenue	(Jee-in-gwaw-mun Jee-eh)
Lianhuachi Road	(Lee-in-hwah-chee Luu)
Qianmen Street	(Chee-in-mun Dah-jee-eh)
Sanlihe Road	(Sahn-lee-huh Luu)
Wangfujing Street	(Wahng-fuu-jeeng Dah-jee-eh)
Wanshou Road	(Wahn-show Luu)
Wukesong Road	(Wuu-kuh-soong Luu)
Xianwumen Street	(Shee-in-wuu-mun Dah-jee-eh)
Xidan Bei Road	(She-dahn Bay Luu)
Xinhua Nan Road	(Sheen-hwah Nahn Luu)
Xinjiekou Road	(Sheen-jee-eh-koe Luu)
Xisi Bei Street	(She-suh Bay Jee-eh)
Xizhimen Street	(She-jr-mun Jee-eh)
Xuanwumen Street	(Shwen-wuu-mun Dah-jee-eh)
Xueyuan Road	(Shu-eh-ywen Luu)
Yongdingmen Nei Avenue	(Yoong-deeng-mun Nay Dah-jee-eh)
Zhushikou Road	(Juu-shr-koe Luu)
Zizhuyuan Road	(Dzu-juu-ywen Luu)

Guangzhou Landmarks

Chen Clan Academy	Chen Jia Su (Chun Jee-ah Suu)

Children's Palace	Haizimen-de Gongdian (High-dzu-mun-duh Goong-dee-in)
Dongshan Park	Dongshan Gongyuan (Doong-shahn Goong-ywen)
Friendship Store	Youyi Shang Dian (Yoe-ee Shahng Dee-in)
Guangdong Provincial Museum	Guangdong Shengli Bowuguan (Gwahng-doong Shuung-lee Bwo-wuu-gwahn)
Guangzhou Cultural Park	Guangzhou Wenhua Gongyuan (Gwahng-joe Wun-hwah Goong-ywen)
Guangzhou Uprising Memorial	Guangzhou Gemin Jinian (Gwahng-joe Guu-meen Jee-nee-in)
Guangzhou Zoo	Guangzhou Dongwuyuan (Gwahng-joe Doong-wuu-ywen)
Haizhu Square	Haizhu Guangchang (High-juu Gwahng-chahng)
Hall of Arts and Crafts	Meishu Gongyipin Guan (May-shuu goong-ee-peen Gwahn)

History Museum	Lishi Bowuguan (Lee-shr Bwo-wuu-gwahn)
Liuhua Park	Liuhua Gongyuan (Leo-hwah Goong-ywen)
Lu Lake	Lu Hu (Luu Huu)
Martyrs' Memorial Park	Xunnanzhe Jinian Gongyuan (Shwun-nahn-juu Jee-nee-in Goong-ywen)
Nanfang Department Store	Nanfang Baihuoshangchang (Nahn-fahng Buy-hwaw-shahng-chahng)
Pearl River	Zhu Jiang (Juu Jee-ahng)
Peasant Institute	Nongmin Yanjiusuo (Noong-meen Yahn-jew-swaw)
People's Stadium	Renmin Tiyuchang (Wren-meen Tee-yuu-chahng)
Provincial Museum	Shengli Bowuguan (Shuung-lee Bwo-wuu-gwahn)
Shamian Island	Shamian (Shah-mee-in)
South China Botanical Gardens	Huanan Zhiwu Yuan (Hwah-nahn Jr-wuu Ywen)

Sun Yatsen Memorial Hall	Sun Zhongshan Jinian Guan (Swun Joong-shahn Jee-nee-in Gwahn)
Tower Overlooking Sea	Zhen Hai Lou (Jun High Low)
Yuexiu Park	Yuexiu Gongyuan (Yu-eh-sheo Goong-ywen)

Shopping Districts in Guangzhou

Beijing Road (Bay-jeeng Luu)

Renmin Road (Wren-meen Luu)

Guangzhou's Main Streets

Baoyuan Road (Bow-ywen Luu)

Beijing Road (Bay-jeeng Luu)

Binjiang Road (Bin-jee-ahng Luu)

Daxin Road (Dah-sheen Luu)

Dengfeng Road (Duung-fuung Luu)

Dengfeng (Dao) Road (Duung-fuung [Dow] Luu)

Gongye Road (Goong-yeh Luu)

Guangzhou Road (Gwahng-joe Luu)

Guangzhou Qiyu Road (Gwahng-joe Chee-yuu Luu)

Guigang Road (Gway-gahng Luu)

Haizhu (Dao) Road (High-juu [Dow] Luu)

Heping Road (Huh-peeng Luu)

Hongyun Road (Hoong-ywun Luu)

Huangsha Road (Hwahng-shah Luu)

Huanshi (Dao) Road (Hwahn-shr [Dow] Luu)

Jianglan Road (Jee-ahng-lahn Luu)

Jiefang Road (Jee-eh-fahng Luu)

Liuersan Road (Leo-urr-sahn Luu)

Liwan Road (Lee-wahn Luu)

Longlinxia Road (Loong-leen-shee-ah Luu)

Nanhua Road (Nahn-hwah Luu)

Qianjin Road (Chee-in-jeen Luu)

Qiyi Road (Chee-ee Luu)

Renmin Bei Road (Wren-meen Bay Luu)

Renmin Nan Road (Wren-meen Nahn Luu)

Shamian Road (Shah-mee-in Luu)

Shuguang Road (Shuu-gwahng Luu)

Wenchang Road (Wun-chahng Luu)

Wende Road (Wun-duh Luu)

Xiangqun Road (Shee-ahng-chwun Luu)

Xiangyang Road (Shee-ahng-yahng Luu)

Xianlie Road (Shee-in-lee-eh Luu)

Xicun Road (She-tswun Luu)

Xihua Road (She-hwah Luu)

Xiuli Road (Sheo-lee Luu)

Yanan Road (Yah-nahn Luu)

Yanjiang Road (Yahn-jee-ahng Luu)

Yide Road (Ee-duh Luu)

Yuexiu Road (Yu-eh-sheo Luu)

Zhongshan (Dao) Road (Joong-shahn [Dow] Luu)

Landmarks in Shanghai

The Bund	Waitan Zhongshan Road	(Wigh-tahn) (Joong-shahn Luu)
Fuxing Park	Fuxing Gongyuan	(Fuu-sheeng Goong-ywen)
Jade Buddha Temple	Yufosi	(Yuu-fwo-suh)
Longhua Temple and Pagoda	Longhua Miao He Ta	(Loong-hwah Mee-ow Huh Tah)
Lu Xun Memorial Museum	Luxun Jinian Guan	(Luu-shwun Jee-nee-in Gwahn)
Museum of Natural History	Ziran Lishi Bowuguan	(Dzu-rahn Lee-shr Bwo-wuu-gwahn)
Old Town	Shanghai Jiu Shi	(Shahng-high Jeo Shr)
People's Park and Square	Renmin Guangchang	(Wren-meen Gwahng-chahng)
Shanghai Acrobatic Theater	Shanghai Zajiyan Juyuan	(Shahng-high Zah-jee-yahn Juu-ywen)

(Continued)

Landmarks in Shanghai (Continued)

English	Chinese (Pinyin)	Pronunciation
Shanghai Children's Palace	Shanghai Shaonian Gong	(Shahng-high Shah-aw-nee-in Goong)
Shanghai Exhibition Center	Shanghai Janlan Guan	(Shahng-high Jahn-lahn Gwahn)
Shanghai Museum of Art and History	Shanghai Bowugaun-de Yishu he Lishi	(Shahng-high Bwo-wuu-gwahn-duh Ee-shuu huh Lee-shr)
Sun Yatsen Residence	Sun Zhongshan Guju	(Swun Joong-shahn Guu-juu)
Tomb of Song Qingling	Song Qingling Fenmu	(Soong Cheeng-leeng Fin-muu)
Workers' Cultural Palace	Gongren Wenhua Gong	(Goong-wren Wun-hwah Goong)
Xijiao Park	Xi Jiao Gongyuan	(She Jee-ow Goong-ywen)
Yu Garden	Yu Yuan	(Yuu Ywen)

Special Clubs

Friendship Store
Youyi Shang Dian
(Yoe-ee Shahng Dee-in)

Service Center for Overseas Traders (SCOT)
Wai Shang Fuwu Zhongxin
(Wigh Shahng Fuu-wuu Joong-sheen)

Shanghai Intl Golf and Country Club
Shanghai Guoji Gaoerfu he Nongcun Julebo
(Shahng-high Gwaw-jee Gow-urr-fuu huh Noong-tswun
  Juu-luh-bwo)

Shopping Districts in Shanghai

Huaihai Road (Hwie-high Luu)

Nanjing Road (Nahn-jeeng Luu)、

Shanghai's Main Streets

Anyuan Road (Ahn-ywen Luu)

Beijing Road (Bay-jeeng Luu)

Caoyang Road (Tsow-yahng Luu)

Changle Road (Chahng-luh Luu)

Changning Road (Chahng-neeng Luu)

Changshou Road (Chahng-show Luu)

Changshu Road (Chahng-shuu Luu)

Changzhi Road (Chahng-jr Luu)

Chao Xi Road (Chow She Luu)

Chengdu Road (Chuung-duu Luu)

Chongqing Road (Choong-cheeng Luu)

Daming Road (Dah-meeng Luu)

Fujian Road (Fuu-jee-in Luu)

Fuman Road (Fuu-mahn Luu)

Fuzhou Road (Fuu-joe Luu)

Gonghexin Road (Goong-huh-sheen Luu)

Haining Road (High-neeng Luu)

Henan Road (Huh-nahn Luu)

Hengshan Road (Huung-shahn Luu)

Huaihai Road (Hwie-high Luu)

Huashan Road (Hwah-shahn Luu)

Jiangning Road (Jee-ahng-neeng Luu)

Kending Road (Kin-deeng Luu)

Luban Road (Luu-bahn Luu)

Lujiabin Road (Luu-jee-ah-bin Luu)

Maoming Road (Mou-meeng Luu)

Nanjing Road (Nahn-jeeng Luu)

Qiaozhou Road (Chee-ow-joe Luu)

Renmin Road (Wren-meen Luu)

Ruijin Road (Rway-jeen Luu)

Shimen Road (Shr-mun Luu)

Sichuan Road (Suh-chwahn Luu)

Tianmu Road (Tee-in-muu Luu)

Wanhangdu Road (Wahn-hahng-duu Luu)

Weihai Road (Way-high Luu)

Wuning Road (Wuu-neeng Luu)

Xinzha Road (Sheen-jah Luu)

Xizang Road (She-zahng Luu)

Xujiahui Road (Shu-jee-ah-hway Luu)

Yanan Road (Yah-nahn Luu)

Yanan Xi Road (Yah-nahn She Luu)

Yuyao Road (Yuu-yow Luu)

Zhaojiabin Road (Jow-jee-ah-bin Luu)

Zhejiang Road (Juh-jee-ahng Luu)

Zhonghua Road (Joong-hwah Luu)

Zhongshan Road (Joong-shahn Luu)

Zhongshan Bei Road (Joong-shahn Bay Luu)

Zhongshan Nan Road (Joong-shahn Nahn Luu)

PART TWO

Communicating in Chinese

Common Expressions

I, me	wo	(waw)
mine	wo-de	(waw-duh)
you	ni	(nee)
your	ni-de	(nee-duh)
you (plural)	nimen	(nee-mun)
your (plural)	nimen-de	(nee-mun-duh)
he, she, it	ta	(tah)
his, hers, its	ta-de	(tah-duh)
we, us	women	(waw-mun)
our	women-de	(waw-mun-duh)
they, them	tamen	(tah-mun)
their, theirs	tamen-de	(tah-mun-duh)
Hello.	Ni hao.	(Nee how.)

Ni hao, or *nin hao* (neen how), a more polite form, may be used as the equivalent of "good morning," "good afternoon," and "good evening," but there are also special terms for these expressions.

Good morning.	Zaoshang hao.	(Zow-shahng how.)
Good afternoon.	Xiawu hao.	(Shee-ah-wuu how.)
Good evening.	Wanshang hao.	(Wahn-shahng how.)
How are you?	Nin hao ma?	(Neen how mah?)
Fine; thank you.	Hen hao; xiexie.	(Hin how; she-eh-she-eh.)
And you?	Ni ne?	(Nee nuh?)
Good night.	Wan an.	(Wahn ahn.)
Good-bye.	Zai-jian.	(Zigh-jee-in.)
See you tomorrow.	Mingtian jian.	(Meeng-tee-in jee-in.)
Please	Qing	(Cheeng)
Thank you	xie xie	(she-eh she-eh)*
You're welcome.	Bu xie.	(Buu shee-eh.)

---

* At a normal speaking speed, this sounds like "shay shay."

Don't mention it.	Bu keqi.
	Meiyou
	  guanxi.
		(Buu kuh-chee.);
		(May-yoe
		  gwahn-she.)

Welcome. (to guests)	Huanying.	(Hwahn-eeng.)
That's right.	Duile.	(Dway-luh.)
That's all right.	Mei guanxi.	(May gwahn-she.)
All right; okay	hao hao ba	(how); (how bah)
That's wrong.	Bu dui.	(Buu dway.)

Excuse me.
  (May I trouble
  you?)
	Mafan ni.	(Mah-fahn nee.)

Excuse me. (May I ask . . . ?)	Qing wen. Duibuqi.	(Cheeng wun.); (Dway-buu-chee.)

Excuse me.
  (make way)
	Qing rang yi
	  rang.
		(Cheeng rahng ee
		  rahng.)

Excuse me! (to get attention)	Lao jia!	(Lou jee-ah!)
I'm sorry; I apologize.	Duibuqi.	(Dway-buu-chee.)

I'm very sorry.	Hen
	  baoqian.
		(Hin
		  bow-chee-in.)

Please hurry!	Qing gankuai!	(Cheeng gahn-kwie!)
Good.	Hao.	(How.)
Very Good.	Hen hao.	(Hin how.)
Excellent!	Hao ji le!	(How jee luh!)
Congratulations.	Zhuhe ni. Gong xi.	(Juu-huh nee.); (Goong she.)
Yes, I agree; correct.	Shi; dui.	(Shr); (dway.)
No. (not so)	Bu shi.	(Buu shr.)

As mentioned, just plain "yes" and "no" are not used as commonly in Chinese as they are in English. In fact, some purists say the two words really don't exist in Chinese.

"No," or the negative, is usually expressed by putting the negative indicator *bu* (buu) in front of verbs and adjectives and by prefacing sentences with the negative indicator *mei* (may).

"Yes," or the positive, is generally expressed by repeating the verb.

Yes. (there is/ there are/ I have)	You.	(Yoe.)
That's no good.	Bu hao.	(Buu how.)
I understand.	Wo dong.	(Waw doong.)

I don't understand.	Wo bu dong.	(Waw buu doong.)
Do you understand?	Dong ma?	(Doong mah?)
Did you understand?	Ni ming bai le ma?	(Nee meeng buy luh mah?)
I'm not sure.	Wo bu qingchu.	(Waw buu cheeng-chuu.)
Please repeat that.	Qing ni zaishuo yibian.	(Cheeng nee zigh-shwaw ee-bee-in.)
Do you speak English?	Ni hui Yingwen ma?	(Nee hway Eeng-wun mah?);
	Ni dong bu dong Yingwen?	(Nee doong buu doong Eeng-wun?)
Where are you from?	Ni shi cong nar lai-de?	(Nee shr tsoong nah-urr lie-duh?)
I'm from _____.	Wo shi _____ lai-de.	(Waw shr _____ lie-duh.)
I know.	Wo zhidao.	(Waw jr-dow.)
I don't know.	Wo bu zhidao.	(Waw buu jr-dow.)

fast	kuai	(kwie)
slow	man	(mahn)
Please speak more slowly.	Qing ni shuo man dian.	(Cheeng nee shwaw mahn dee-in.)
I need an interpreter.	Wo xuyao fanyi.	(Waw shu-yow fahn-ee.)
I want to study Chinese.	Wo yao xue xi Zhongwen.	(Waw yow shu-eh she Joong-wun.)
Please speak in Chinese.	Qing jiang Zhongwen.	(Cheeng jee-ahng Joong-wun.)
Is it all right?	Hao le ma? Xing le ma?	(How luh mah?); (Sheeng luh mah?)
It doesn't matter.	Mei guan xi.	(May gwahn she.)
Is that so?	Jiu na xie?	(Jeo nah she-eh?)
I don't want it.	Wo bu yao.	(Waw buu yow.)
I think so.	Wo xiang shi-de.	(Waw shee-ahng shr-duh.)
I don't think so.	Wo bu renwei zheyang.	(Waw buu wren-way juh-yahng.)

| Just a moment. | Deng ye xia. | (Duung yeh shee-ah.) |
| No problem. | Mei wenti. | (May wun-tee.) |

Key Words and Example Sentences

this	zhe	(juh);
	zhei	(jay)
that	na	(nah);
	nei	(nay)
who	shui	(shway)
what	shenme	(shuun-muh)
when	shenme shihou	(shuun-muh shr-hoe)
where	nali	(nah-lee);
	nar	(nah-urr)
why	weishenme	(way-shuun-muh)
how	duo	(dwaw);
	duome	(dwaw-muh);
	zenme	(zen-muh);
	jige	(jee-guh)
which	nei	(nay);
	na	(nah)

This   Zhe (Juh); Zhei (Jay)

This is mine.
Zhe shi wo-de.
(Juh shr waw-duh.)

Please take this with you.
Qing ba zhe-ge gei wo.
(Cheeng bah juh-guh gay waw.)

How much is this?
Zhe shi duoshao?
(Juh shr dwaw-shah-oh?)

This is very good.
Zhe hen hao.
(Juh hin how.)

What is this?
Zhe shi shenme?
(Juh shr shuun-muh?)

That   Na (Nah); Nei (Nay)

What is that?
Na shi shenme?
(Nah shr shuun-muh?)

That's right.
Na shi dui-de.
(Nah shr dway-duh.)

That's too much.
Na shi tai duo-le.
(Nah shr tie dwaw-luh.)

That's my luggage.
Na shi wo-de xingli.
(Nah shr waw-duh sheeng-lee.)

Will that be all?
Na kuai hao-le ma?
(Nah kwie how-luh mah?)

Who was that?
Na shi shei?
(Nah shr shay?)

May I see that?
Wo kerikan na-ge ma?
(Waw kuh-rr-kahn nah-guh mah?)

Who   Shui (Shway)

Who are you?
Ni shi shei?
(Nee shr shay?)

Who is that person?
Ni-ge ren shi she?
(Nee-guh wren shr shuh?)

Who is going?
Shei zao-le?
(Shay zow-luh?)

Who wants to go?
Shei xiang qu?
(Shay shee-ahng chu?)

Who is first?
Shei shi-de yi-ge?
(Shay shr-duh ee-guh?)

What   Shenme (Shuun-muh)

What is that?
Na shi shenme?
(Nah shr shuun-muh?)

What time is it?
Ji dian-le?
(Jee dee-in-luh?)

What shall we do?
Women jiang yao gan shenme?
(Waw-mun jee-ahng yow gahn shuun-muh?)

What would you like to do?
Ni xi huan gan shenme?
(Nee she hwahn gahn shuun-muh?)

I don't know what to do.
Wo bu zhidao zeng mo gan.
(Waw buu jr-dow zuung mwo gahn.)

Please tell me what to do.
Qing gaosu wo gan shenme.
(Cheeng gow-suu waw gahn shuun-muh.)

What is that called?
Na you shenme mingzi?
(Nah yoe shuun-muh meeng-dzu?)

What is this street?
Zhe shi neitiao jie?
(Juh shr nay-tee-ow jee-eh?)

When   Shenme shihou
(Shuun-muh shr-hoe)

When are you going?
Ni shenme shihou qu?
(Nee shuun-muh shr-hoe chu?)

When do you want to go?
Ni shenme shihou xiang qu?
(Nee shuun-muh shr-hoe shee-ahng chu?)

When will you be back?
Ni shenme shihou huilai?
(Nee shuun-muh shr-hoe hway-lie?)

When will it be ready?
Shenme shihou zhunbei hao?
(Shuun-muh shr-hoe juwun-bay how?)

When did you arrive?
Ni shenme shihou daolai?
(Nee shuun-muh shr-hoe dow-lie?)

When are you leaving?
Ni shenme shihou likai?
(Nee shuun-muh shr-hoe lee-kigh?)

Where   Nali (Nah-lee); Nar (Nah-urr)

Where are you going?
Ni yao qu nali?
(Nee yow chu nah-lee?)

Where do you want to go?
Ni xiang qu nali?
(Nee shee-ahng chu nah-lee?)

Where is it?
Ta zai nali?
(Tah zigh nah-lee?)

Where can I find _____?
Zai nali wo keyi zaodao _____?
(Zigh nah-lee waw kuh-ee zow-dow _____?

Where is Mr. Lee?
Li Xiansheng zai nali?
(Lee Shee-in-shuung zigh nah-lee?)

I don't know where he is.
Wo bu zhidao ta zai nali.
(Waw buu jr-dow tah zigh nah-lee.)

Where is _____?
_____ zai nar?
(_____ zigh nah-urr?)

Is it far?
Yuan bu yuan?
(Ywen buu ywen?)

Is it near here?
Li zher jin ma?
(Lee juhr jeen mah?)

Can I walk there?
Wo keyi zoulu ma?
(Waw kuh-ee zoe-luu mah?)

Locations

airport	jichang	(jee-chahng)
bus station (central)	qiche zongzhan	(chee-chuh zoong-jahn)
bus stop	qiche zhan	(chee-chuh jahn)
subway station	ditie zhan	(dee-tee-eh jahn)
train station	huoche zhan	(hwaw-chuh jahn)
ticket office	shoupiao chu	(show-pee-ow chuu)

Why   Weishenme (Way-shuun-muh)

Why are you upset?
Ni wei shenme bu gaoxing?
(Nee way shuun-muh buu gow-sheeng?)

Why do you need that?
Ni wei shenme xurao na-ge?
(Nee way shuun-muh shu-rou nah-guh?)

Why can't you go with me?
Ni wei shenme bu hewo qu?
(Nee way shuun-muh buu huh-waw chu?)

Why have we stopped?
Weishenme women tingxia?
(Way-shuun-muh waw-mun teeng-shee-ah?)

How   Duo (Dwaw);
Duome (Dwaw-muh);
Zenme (Zen-muh)

How much?
Duo shao?
(Dwaw shah-oh?)

How much is this?
Zhe shi duo shao?
(Juh shr dwaw shah-oh?)

How does this work?
Zhe gongzuo zenme zuo?
(Juh goong-zwaw zen-muh zwaw?)

I don't know how to do it.
Wo bu zhidao zenme gan.
(Waw buu jr-dow zen-muh gahn.)

Please show me how.
Qing rung wo kankan duoshao.
(Cheeng ruung waw kahn-kahn dwaw-shou.)

How long will it take?
Zhe yao duo chang?
(Juh yow dwaw chahng?)

How far is it?
Li zhe duo yuan?
(Lee juh dwaw ywen?)

How many are there?
Ni li you duoshao?
(Nee lee yoe dwaw-shou?)

How many do you want?
Ni xiang yao duoshao?
(Nee shee-ahng yow dwaw-shou?)

Whose   Shui-de (Shway-duh)

Whose book is this?
Zhe ben shu shi shui-de?
(Juh bin shuu shr shway-duh?)

Whose house are we going to?
Women yao qu shi de jia?
(Waw-mun yow chu shr duh jee-ah?)

Which   Na (Nah); Nei (Nay)

Which one?
Na yi-ge?
(Nah yee-guh?)

Which kind?
Na yang?
(Nah yahng?)

Which one is yours?
Na yi-ge shi ni-de?
(Nah ee-guh shr nee-duh?)

Which one do you want?
Na yi-ge ni xiang yao?
(Nah ee-guh nee shee-ahng yow?)

Please show me which one.
Qing gei wo kankan shi na yi-ge.
(Cheeng gay waw kahn-kahn shr nah ee-guh.)

Which way shall we go?
Women keyi zao na yi tiao lu?
(Waw-mun kuh-ee zow nah ee tee-ow luu?)

Buy　Mai (My)

I want to buy some shoes.
Wo xiang mai xie.
(Waw shee-ahng my she-eh.)

Where can I buy an umbrella?
Nali wo keyi mai rusan?
(Nah-lee waw kuh-ee my ruuh-sahn?)

I bought it at a department store.
Wo cong ye-ge shangdian mai-de.
(Waw tsoong yuh-guh shahng-dee-in my-duh.)

What do you want to buy?
Ni xiang mai sheng mo?
(Nee shee-ahng my shuung mwo?)

Come　Lai (Lie)

Please come with me.
Qing he wo guo lai.
(Cheeng huh waw gwaw lie.)

When did you come?
Shenme shihou ni lai?
(Shuun-muh shr-hoe nee lie?)

Are you coming with us?
Ni he women yeqi lai ma?
(Nee huh waw-mun yeh-chee lie mah?)

What time shall I come?
Shenme shihou wa lai?
(Shuun-muh shr-hoe waw lie?)

Can you come tomorrow?
Ni neng mingtian lai ma?
(Nee nuung meeng-tee-in lie mah?)

Drink (noun) Yinliao (Een-lee-ow)

What kind of drinks do you have?
Ni xiang he shenme?
(Nee shee-ahng huh shuun-muh?)

What kind of drink is that?
Zhe shi shenme yinliao?
(Juh shr shuun-muh een-lee-ow?)

I cannot drink alcoholic drinks.
Wo bu he jiu.
(Wah buu huh jeo.)

Let's go get a drink.
Women qu he jiu.
(Waw-mun chu huh jeo.)

Drink (verb) He (Huh)

What are you drinking?
Ni he shenme ne?
(Nee huh shuun-muh nuh?)

What do you want to drink?
Ni xiang he shenme?
(Nee shee-ahng huh shuun-muh?)

Do you want something to drink?
Ni xiang he dian yinliao ma?
(Nee shee-ahng huh dee-in een-lee-ow mah?)

I want to drink something cold.
Wo xiang he dian liang-de yinliao.
(Waw shee-ahng huh dee-in lee-ahng-duh
een-lee-ow.)

I cannot drink very much.
Wo bu neng he tai duo.
(Waw buu nuung huh tie dwaw.)

Eat   Chi (Chee)

What do you want to eat?
Ni xiang chi shenme?
(Nee shee-ahng chee shuun-muh?)

Where shall we eat?
Women qu nali chi?
(Waw-mun chu nah-lee chee?)

Have you eaten already?
Ni yijin chi-le ma?
(Nee ee-jeen chee-luh mah?)

What did you eat last night?
Zuo tian wanshang ni chi-de shenme?
(Zwaw tee-in wahn-shahng nee chee-duh
shuun-muh?)

Have you eaten this before?
Zai zhe zhiqian ni chi guo ma?
(Zigh juh jr-chee-in nee chee gwaw mah?)

What time do we eat?
Women shenme shi jian chifan?
(Waw-mun shuun-muh shr jee-in chee-fahn?)

Let's go eat.
Rang wo women qu chifan.
(Rahng waw waw-mun chu chee-fahn.)

I can't eat this.
Wo bu neng chi zhe-ge.
(Waw buu nuung chee juh-guh.)

I can't eat all of this.
Wa bu neng chi wang suo you-de.
(Wah buu nuung chee wahng swaw yoe-duh.)

Enough   Goule (Go-luh)

Is this enough?
Zhe xie gou-le ma?
(Juh she-eh go-luh mah?)

That's enough.
Na xie gou-le.
(Nah she-eh go-luh.)

Have you had enough?
Ni chi gou-le ma?
(Nee chee go-luh mah?)

A little   Yidianr dianr
(Ee-dee-in-urr dee-in-urr)

Just a little, please.
Jiu yidianr dianr.
(Jeo ee-dee-in-urr dee-in-urr.)

Please take a little more.
Qing duo na yidianr.
(Cheeng dwaw nah ee-dee-in-urr.)

Too much   Tai duole (Tie dwaw-luh)

That's too much.
Na xie tai duo-le.
(Nah she-eh tie dwaw-luh.)

Give   Gei (Gay)

Please give this to Mr. Wong.
Qing ba zhe xie song gei Wang Xiansheng.
(Cheeng bah juh she-eh soong gay Wahng Shee-in-shuung.)

He gave it to me.
Ta gei wo-de.
(Tah gay waw-duh.)

Please give me a little more time.
Qing gei wo yidian shi jian.
(Cheeng gay waw ee-dee-in shr jee-in.)

I will give it to him/her.
Wo yao ba zhe-ge gei ta.
(Waw yow bah juh-guh gay tah.)

Go   Qu (Chu)

Are you going?
Ni qu ma?
(Nee chu mah?)

Where are you going?
Ni qu nali?
(Nee chu nah-lee?)

When do you want to go?
Ni shenme shihou qu?
(Nee shuun-muh shr-hoe chu?)

Can you go with me?
Ni neng he wo yiqi qu ma?
(Nee nuung huh waw ee-chee chu mah?)

I cannot go today.
Wo jintian bu neng qu.
(Waw jeen-tee-in buu nuung chu.)

I don't want to go there.
Wo bu xiang qu nali.
(Waw buu shee-ahng chu nah-lee.)

I want to go to a shopping district.
Wo xiang zhi jie qu bai dongxi.
(Waw shee-ahng jr jee-eh chu buy doong-she.)

Have You (Yoe)

I don't have it.
Wo mei you.
(Waw may yoe.)

Do you have it?
Ni you ma?
(Nee yoe mah?)

How many do you have?
Ni you duo shao?
(Nee yoe dwaw shou?)

I don't have enough money.
Wo mei you na mo duo qian.
(Waw may yoe nah mwo dwaw chee-in.)

I have a headache.
Wo you dian toutong.
(Waw yoe dee-in toe-toong.)

Do you have English language books?
Ni you Yingyu shu ma?
(Nee yoe Eeng-yuu shuu mah?)

Do you have any fresh fruit?
Ni you shenme xinxian shuiguo ma?
(Nee yoe shuun-muh sheen-shee-in shway-gwaw mah?)

Is there any fresh fruit?
Zhe you xinxian shuiguo ma?
(Juh yoe sheen-shee-in shway-gwaw mah?)

Hear   Ting (Teeng)

I cannot hear you.
Wo ting bu jian ni-de sheng yin.
(Waw teeng buu jee-in nee-duh shuung een.)

Can you hear me?
Ni neng ting jian wo-de sheng yin ma?
(Nee nuung teeng jee-in waw-duh shuung een mah?)

What did you hear?
Ni zai ting shenmo?
(Nee zigh teeng shuun-mwo?)

Know   Zhidao (Jr-dow)
   Know (a person or place)
   Renshi (Wren-shr)

I know.
Wo zhidao.
(Waw jr-dow.)

I don't know.
Wa bu zhidao.
(Waw buu jr-dow.)

Do you know Mrs. Hong?
Ni renshi Hong Xiaojie ma?
(Nee wren-shr Hoong Shee-ow-jee-eh mah?)

No, I don't know her.
Bu, wo bu renshi ta.
(Buu, waw buu wren-shr tah.)

I don't know what to do.
Wo bu zhidao gan shenme.
(Waw buu jr-dow gahn shuun-muh.)

Like Xihuan (She-hwahn)

Do you like it?
Xihuan ma?
(She-hwahn mah?)

I don't like it.
Bu xihuan.
(Buu she-hwahn.)

Do you like Western food?
Ni xihuan Xi can ma?
(Nee she-hwahn She tsahn mah?)

Yes, I like it.
Xihuan.
(She-hwahn.)

I like Chinese food.
Zhong can xihuan.
(Joong tsahn she-hwahn.)

Look/see Kan (Kahn)

May I look at it?
Wo neng kan ma?
(Waw nuung kahn mah?)

I want to see _____.
Wo yao kan _____.
(Waw yow kahn _____.)

Mistake   Cuowu (Tswaw-wuu);
Cuoshi (Tswaw-shr)

I think that's a mistake.
Wo xiang na shi-ge cuowu.
(Waw shee-ahng nah shr-guh tswaw-wuu.)

He made a mistake.
Ta zuo-le yijian cuoshi.
(Tah zwaw-luh ee-jee-in tswaw-shr.)

I made a mistake.
Wo zuo-le yijian cuoshi.
(Waw zwaw-luh ee-jee-in tswaw-shr.)

Once more   Zaiyici (Zigh-ee-tsu)

One more time, please.
Qing, zaiyici.
(Cheeng, zigh-ee-tsu.)

I want to go to China once more.
Wo xiang zai qu yici Zhongguo.
(Waw shee-ahng zigh chu ee-tsu Joong-gwaw.)

Read   Kan (Kahn); Du (Duu);
Shuo (Shwaw)

Can you read this?
Ni neng du (kan) zhe-ge ma?
(Nee nuung duu [kahn] juh-guh mah?)

Please read it out loud.
Qing da sheng du.
(Cheeng dah shuung duu.)

Read it to me.
Du zhe-ge gaiwo.
(Duu juh-guh guy-waw.)

Have you read this book?
Ni du guo zhe-ben shu ma?
(Nee duu gwaw juh-bin shuu mah?)

I cannot read Chinese.
Wo bu hui kan Zhongwen.
(Waw buu hway kahn Joong-wun.)

Return (Go back)   Hui (Hway); Huilai (Hway-lie); Huan (Hwahn)

I will return by five o'clock.
Wo jiang wu dian zhong huilai.
(Waw jee-ahng wuu dee-in joong hway-lie.)

Please return by four o'clock.
Qing si dian zhong huan.
(Cheeng suh dee-in joong hwahn.)

I must return to the United States tomorrow.
Wo mingtian bixu hui Meiguo.
(Waw Meeng-tee-in bee-shu hway May-gwaw.)

Mr. Lee has returned to China.
Lee Xiansheng yijing hui Zhongguo.
(Lee Shee-in-shuung ee-jeeng hway Joong-gwaw.)

They haven't returned yet.
Tamen hai mei huan na.
(Tah-mun high may hwahn nah.)

Return (Give back)   Huan (Hwahn)

Please return this to Miss Lee.
Qing ba zhe-ge huan gei Lee Xiaojie.
(Cheeng bah juh-guh hwahn gay Lee
Shee-ow-jee-eh.)

I returned it yesterday.
Wo mingtian huan.
(Waw meeng-tee-in hwahn.)

Please fill this out and return it to me.
Qing tian hao zhe-ge biao, zai huan gei wo.
(Cheeng tee-in how juh-guh bee-ow, zigh hwahn gay
waw.)

Say   Shuo (Shwaw)

What did you say?
Ni shuo shen mo?
(Nee shwaw shuun mwo?)

What did he say?
Ta shuo shen mo?
(Tah shwaw shuun mwo?)

I cannot say for sure.
Wo shuo de bu que ding.
(Wah shwaw duh buu chu-uh deeng.)

What should I say?
Wo yingai shuo shen mo?
(Waw een-guy shwaw shuun mwo?)

See   Kan (Kahn)

Did you see the Great Wall?
Ni kan guo Chang Cheng?
(Nee kahn gwaw Chahng Chuung?)

What do you want to see?
Ni xiang kan shenme?
(Nee shee-ahng kahn shuun-muh?)

I would like to see Mr. Zhang.
Wo xiang kankan Zhang Xiansheng.
(Waw shee-ahng kahn-kahn Jahng Shee-in-shuung.)

I cannot see it.
Wo kan bu jian.
(Waw kahn buu jee-in.)

Have you seen this?
Ni kan guo zhe-ge ma?
(Nee kahn gwaw juh-guh mah?)

Sleep   Shuijiao (Shway-jee-ow)

What time did you go to sleep?
Ji dian ni qu shujiao?
(Jee dee-in nee chu shuu-jee-ow?)

How long did you sleep?
Ni shui duo cheng shijian?
(Nee shway dwaw chuung shr-jee-in?)

I must get some sleep.
Wo bixu shui yi hui jiao.
(Waw bee-shu shway ee hway jee-ow.)

He is still asleep.
Ta reng ran zai shuijiao.
(Tah ruung rahn zigh shway-jee-ow.)

Did you sleep well?
Ni shui-de hao ma?
(Nee shway-duh how mah?)

Speak   Shuohua (Shwaw-hwah); Jianghua (Jee-ahng-hwah)

May I speak to Mr Wang?
Wo keyi he Wang Xiansheng shuorhua ma?
(Waw kuh-ee huh Wahng Shee-in-shuung shwaw-urr-hwah mah?)

To whom did you wish to speak?
Ni xiang he shei shuohua?
(Nee shee-ahng huh shay shwaw-hwah?)

Please speak slowly.
Qing jiang man yidian.
(Cheeng jee-ahng mahn ee-dee-in.)

I cannot speak Chinese.
Wo bu hui jiang Zhongwen.
(Waw buu hway jee-ahng Joong-wun.)

Excuse me, do you speak English?
Duibuqi, ni jiang Yingyu ma?
(Dway-buu-chee, nee jee-ahng Eeng-yuu mah?)

Walk   Zou (Zoe)

Let's walk.
Rang women zouzou.
(Rahng waw-mun zoe-zoe.)

Can we walk there?
Women keyi zai nali zouzou ma?
(Waw-mun kuh-ee zigh nah-lee zoe-zoe mah?)

Is it too far to walk?
Zuo lu qu tai yuan-le?
(Zwaw luu chu tie ywen-luh?)

I prefer to walk.
Wo xi huan zuo lu.
(Waw she hwahn zwaw luu.)

It's a long walk.
Zhe shi yici yuan zuo.
(Juh shr ee-tsu ywen zwaw.)

Wait   Deng (Duung)

Please wait just a moment.
Qing deng yi xia.
(Cheeng duung ee shee-ah.)

Please wait for me.
Qing deng deng wo.
(Cheeng duung duung waw.)

Who are you waiting for?
Ni zai deng shei?
(Nee zigh duung shay?)

I am waiting for Mr. Smith.
Wo zai deng Smith Xiansheng.
(Waw zigh duung Smith Shee-in-shuung.)

I'm sorry, I can't wait.
Dubuiqi, wo bu neng deng.
(Duu-bway-chee, waw buu nuung duung.)

Write   Xie (She-eh)

Please write it down.
Qing xie xia lai.
(Cheeng she-eh she-ah lie.)

Please write it in pin yin.
Qing yong pinyin xie.
(Cheeng yoong peen-een she-eh.)

Please write it in Chinese.
Qing yong Zhongwen xie.
(Cheeng yoong Joong-wun she-eh.)

My writing is very poor.
Wo xie zi hen bu hao.
(Waw she-eh dzu hin buu how.)

Who wrote this?
Shei xie de?
(Shay she-eh duh?)

Useful Adjectives

Best   Zuihao (Zway-how)

Which one is best?
Na yi-ge shi zuihao-de?
(Nah ee-guh shr zway-how-duh?)

Better   Geng hao (Guung how)

That one is better.
Na yi-ge geng hao.
(Nah ee-guh guung how.)

Big, large   Da (Dah)

It's too big.
Zhe tei da-le.
(Juh tay dah-luh.)

Cheap   Pianyi (Pee-in-ee)

That looks cheap.
Na-ge kan qilei pianyi.
(Nah-guh kahn chee-lay pee-in-ee.)

Difficult Nan (Nahn)

Chinese is difficult.
Zongwen shi nan xue.
(Joong-wun shr nahn shu-uh.)

Easy Rongyi (Roong-ee)

It's not easy.
Zhe bu shi rong yi-de.
(Juh buu shr roong ee-duh.)

Enough Gou-le (Go-luh)

That is enough.
Zhe gou-le.
(Juh go-luh.)

Expensive Gui (Gway)

That one is too expensive.
Na yi-ge tai gui.
(Nah ee-guh tie gway.)

Fast Kuai (Kwie)

Please don't drive so fast.
Qing bu yao kai-de tei kuai.
(Cheeng buu yow kigh-duh tay kwie.)

Good (well) Hao (How)

I don't feel well.
Wo gou jue bu hao.
(Waw go juu-uh buu how.)

Heavy   Zhong (Joong)

Is my suitcase too heavy?
Wo-de xingli tai zhong-le ma?
(Waw-duh sheeng-lee tie joong-luh mah?)

Less   Shaoxie (Shah-aw-she-eh)

Is this less than that?
Zhe-ge bi na-ge shiao xie?
(Juh-guh bee nah-guh shr-ow she-eh?)

Light (weight)   Qing (Cheeng)

My carry-on bag is very light.
Wo-de beibao shi hen qing-de.
(Waw-duh bay-bow shr hin cheeng-duh.)

Long   Chang (Chahng)

The sleeves are too long.
Xiuzi tai chang-le.
(Sheo-dzu tie chahng-luh.)

Short   Duan (Dwahn)

It is just a short trip.
Zhe shi yici duan-de luxing.
(Juh shr ee-tsu dwahn-duh luu-sheeng.)

Slow   Man (Mahn)

The pace here is very slow.
Zhe li-de bufa shi man-de.
(Juh lee-duh buu-fah shr mahn-duh.)

Small   Xiao (Shee-ow)

I'll take the small one.
Wo jiang na yi-ge xiao-de.
(Waw jee-ahng nah ee-guh shee-ow-duh.)

Too much   Tai duo (Tie dwaw)

That's too much for me.
Zhe xie dui wo shi tei duo-le.
(Juh she-eh dway waw shr tay dwaw-luh.)

Numbers and Counting

Numbers are vital to communication on the most basic level. Without numbers, it is virtually impossible to conceptualize and talk about most of the activities that make up daily life. If you are going to be exposed to Chinese for even a few days, being able to understand and use numbers will be a major asset.

Once you have familiarized yourself with the system, practice reading the phonetic equivalents of 1 through 10 out loud, from top to bottom (*leeng, ee, urr, sahn, suh, wuu, leo, chee, bah, jeo, shr*).

From 10 on, numbers in Chinese follow the same pattern common in other languages. Eleven is ten plus one, 12 is ten plus two, and so on. Twenty is two tens, 30 is three tens, and so forth.

0	ling	(leeng)
1	yi	(ee)*

---

* The pronunciation of *yi* sometimes changes to *yao* (yow) when it is used in higher numbers. For example, 118 is *yao yao ba* (yow yow bah).

2	er	(urr)
	liang	(lee-ahng)*
3	san	(sahn)
4	si	(suh)
5	wu	(wuu)
6	liu	(leo)
7	qi	(chee)
8	ba	(bah)
9	jiu	(jeo)
10	shi	(shr)
11	shiyi	(shr-ee)
12	shier	(shr-urr)
13	shisan	(shr-sahn)
14	shisi	(shr-suh)
15	shiwu	(shr-wuu)
16	shiliu	(shr-leo)

---

* *Liang* is commonly used for expressing 2 in higher numbers.

17	shiqi	(shr-chee)
18	shiba	(shr-bah)
19	shijiu	(shr-jeo)
20	ershi	(urr-shr)
21	ershiyi	(urr-shr-ee)
22	ershier	(urr-shr-urr)
23	ershisan	(urr-shr-sahn)
24	ershisi	(urr-shr:suh)
25	ershiwu	(urr-shr-wuu)
26	ershiliu	(urr-shr-leo)
27	ershiqi	(urr-shr-chee)
28	ershiba	(urr-shr-bah)
29	ershijiu	(urr-shr-jeo)
30	sanshi	(sahn-shr)
31	sanshiyi	(sahn-shr-ee)
32	sanshier	(sahn-shr-urr)
33	sanshisan	(sahn-shr-sahn)

34	sanshisi	(sahn-shr-suh)
35	sanshiwu	(sahn-shr-wuu)
36	sanshiliu	(sahn-shr-leo)
37	sanshiqi	(sahn-shr-chee)
38	sanshiba	(sahn-shr-bah)
39	sanshijiu	(sahn-shr-jeo)
40	sishi	(suh-shr)
50	wushi	(wuu-shr)
60	liushi	(leo-shr)
70	qishi	(chee-shr)
80	bashi	(bah-shr)
90	jiushi	(jeo-shr)
100	yibai	(ee-buy)*
101	yibailingyi	(ee-buy-leeng-ee)
102	yibailinger	(ee-buy-leeng-urr)

---

* *Bai* is the designator for 100.

103	yibailingsan	(ee-buy-leeng-sahn)
104	yibailingsi	(ee-buy-leeng-suh)
105	yibailingwu	(ee-buy-leeng-wuu)
106	yibailingliu	(ee-buy-leeng-leo)
107	yibailingqi	(ee-buy-leeng-chee)
108	yibailingba	(ee-buy-leeng-bah)
109	yibailingjiu	(ee-buy-leeng-jeo)
110	yibailingshi	(ee-buy-leeng-shr)
120	yibaiershi	(ee-buy-urr-shr)
125	yibaiershiwu	(ee-buy-urr-shr-wuu)
130	yibaisanshi	(ee-buy-sahn-shr)
136	yibaisanliu	(ee-buy-sahn-leo)
140	yibaisishi	(ee-buy-suh-shr)
150	yibaiwushi	(ee-buy-wuu-shr)
175	yibaiqishiwu	(ee-buy-chee-shr-wuu)
200	erbai	(urr-buy)

300	sanbai	(sahn-buy)
400	sibai	(suh-buy)
500	wubai	(wuu-buy)
600	lubai	(leo-buy)
700	qibai	(chee-buy)
800	babai	(bah-buy)
1,000	yiqian	(ee-chee-in)*
1,500	yiqianwubai	(ee-chee-in-wuu-buy)
2,000	liangqian	(lee-ahng-chee-in)
2,700	liangqianqibai	(lee-ahng-chee-in-chee-buy)
2,900	liangqianjiubai	(lee-ahng-chee-in-jeo-buy)
3,000	sanqian	(sahn-chee-in)
4,000	siqian	(suh-chee-in)
5,000	wuqian	(wuu-chee-in)

---

* *Qian* is the designator for 1,000.

10,000	yiwan	(ee-wahn)*
11,000	yiwanqian	(ee-wahn-chee-in)
12,000	yiwanliangqian	(ee-wahn-lee-ahng-chee-in)
15,000	yiwanwuqian	(ee-wahn-wuu-chee-in)
20,000	erwan	(urr-wahn)
25,500	erwanwuqianwubai	(urr-wahn-wuu-chee-in-wuu-buy)
30,000	sanwan	(sahn-wahn)
40,000	siwan	(suh-wahn)
50,000	wuwan	(wuu-wahn)
80,000	bawan	(bah-wahn)
100,000	shiwan	(shr-wahn)
150,000	shiwuwan	(shr-wuu-wahn)
200,000	**ershiwan**	**(urr-shr-wahn)**
300,000	**sanshiwan**	**(sahn-shr-wahn)**

---

* *Wan* is the designator for 10,000.

| 500,000 | wushiwan | (wuu-shr-wahn) |
| 1,000,000 | yibaiwan | (ee-buy-wahn) |

Ordinal numbers

Chinese ordinal numbers are created by adding the prefix *di* (dee) to the cardinal numbers.

1st	diyi	(dee-ee)
2nd	dier	(dee-urr)
3rd	disan	(dee-sahn)
4th	disi	(dee-suh)
5th	diwu	(dee-wuu)
10th	dishi	(dee-shr)
11th	dishiyi	(dee-shr-ee)
15th	dishiwu	(dee-shr-wuu)
20th	diershi	(dee-urr-shr)
50th	diwushi	(dee-wuu-shr)
100th	diyibai	(dee-ee-buy)
one half	yi ban	(ee bahn)
one quarter	si fen zhi yi	(suh fin jr ee)

Counting things

As mentioned earlier, there are special indicators or measure words used for counting or giving the number of people and things in Chinese. These special terms go between the numbers and nouns they apply to. The most common of these special words is *ge* (guh), which can be used more or less as a universal indicator.

Other commonly used category measuring words are *ben* (bin), which is used when counting books; *ci* (tsu), used for number of times; *ke* (kuh), which is used for trees; *suo* (swaw), used to refer to buildings and houses; *tiao* (tee-ow), used for long, slender objects like poles and streets; *zhi* (jr), which is used when counting round objects like pencils, sticks, and poles; *zhang* (jahng), used when counting flat things like pieces of paper; *wan* (wahn), used when referring to things that come in bowls; *ping* (peeng), if something is in a bottle; and *kuai* (kwie), used when referring to money. One of the most common of the measure words is *ren* (wren), used for numbering or counting people.

When in doubt, use *ge*. It may not be what is generally used in that particular situation, but it will be understood. Here are some examples:

2 bottles of beer	liang-ping bijiu	(lee-ahng-peeng bee-jeo)
3 glasses of water	san-bei shui	(sahn-bay shway)
5 hamburgers	wu-ge hanbaobao	(wuu-guh hahn-bow-bow)
2 pencils	liang-zhi bi	(lee-ahng-jr bee)

| 4 sheets of paper | si-zhang zhi | (suh-jahng jr) |

| 3 books | san-ben shu | (sahn-bin shuu) |

Please bring me two sheets of paper.
Qing gei wo liang-zhang zhi.
(Cheeng gay waw lee-ahng-jahng jr.)

I have lost two books.
Diule liang ben shu.
(Deo-luh lee-ahng bin shuu.)

I want to buy one book.
Wo xiang mai yi-ben shu.
(Waw shee-ahng my ee-bin shuu.)

Two glasses of water, please.
Qing gei liang-bei shui.
(Cheeng gay lee-ahng-bay shway.)

Two hamburgers, please.
Qing gei liang-ge hanbaobao.
(Cheeng gay lee-ahng-guh hahn-bow-bow.)

Counting people

| person | ren | (wren) |

| people | renmin | (wren-meen) |

| 1 person | yi-ge ren | (ee-guh wren) |

| 2 persons | liang-ge ren | (lee-ahng-guh wren) |

| 3 persons | si-ge ren | (suh-guh wren) |
| 12 persons | shiliang-ge ren | (shr-lee-ahng-guh wren) |

There are two of us.
Zhe you women liang-ge.
(Juh yoe waw-mun lee-ahng-guh.)

We have reservations for five people.
Wo wei wu-ge ren yuding.
(Waw way wuu-guh wren yuu-deeng.)

How many people are in your group?
You duo shao-ge ren zai ni-de zuzhi li?
(Yoe dwaw shou-guh wren zigh nee-duh zuu-jr lee?

This bus will hold 40 people.
Zhe liong qi zhe sheng you sishi-ge ren.
(Juh lee-ong chee juh shuung yoe suh-shr-guh wren.)

Time

Telling time in Chinese is very simple. Instead of numbers plus "o'clock" as in English, the Chinese use numbers plus the word *dian* (dee-in), which basically means "point of time."

time (of day)	shijian	(shr-jee-in)
point in time	dian	(dee-in)
o'clock	zhong	(joong)*

---

* *Zhong* is the Chinese equivalent of "o'clock," but it is seldom used in ordinary conversation.

91

hour	xiaoshi	(shee-ow-shr)
half an hour	ban xiaoshi	(bahn shee-ow-shr)
minute	fen	(fin)
A.M.	shangwu	(shahng-wuu)
P.M.	xiawu	(shee-ah-wuu)
1 o'clock	yi dian	(ee dee-in)
2 o'clock	liang dian	(lee-ahng dee-in)
3 o'clock	san dian	(sahn dee-in)
4 o'clock	si dian	(suh dee-in)
5 o'clock	wu dian	(wuu dee-in)
6 o'clock	liu dian	(leo dee-in)
1:30	yi dian ban	(ee dee-in bahn)
2:30	liang dian ban	(lee-ahng dee-in bahn)
3:30	san dian ban	(sahn dee-in bahn)
1:10	yi dian shifen	(ee dee-in shr-fin)
2:20	liang dian ershifen	(lee-ahng dee-in urr-shr-fin)

3:15   san dian shiwufen   (sahn dee-in shr-wuu-fin)

1 A.M.   zaoshang yi dian   (zow-shahng ee dee-in)

2 A.M.   zaoshang liang dian   (zow-shahng lee-ahng dee-in)

1 P.M.   xiawu yi dian   (shee-ah-wuu ee dee-in)

2 P.M.   xiawu liang dian   (shee-ah-wuu lee-ahng dee-in)

The Chinese divide the 24-hour day into four periods:

early morning   qingzao   (cheeng-zow)
   (midnight to 6 A.M.)

morning   zaoshang   (zow-shahng)
   (6 A.M. to noon)

afternoon   xiawu   (shee-ah-wuu)
   (noon to 6 P.M.)

evening   wanshang   (wahn-shahng)
   (6 P.M. to midnight)

When designating the period of time as well as the hour, both words precede the hour.

1 A.M.   qingzao yi dian
        (cheeng-zow ee dee-in)

8 o'clock in the morning   zaoshang ba dian
        (zow-shang bah dee-in)

1 o'clock in the afternoon		xiawu yi dian (shee-ah-wuu ee dee-in)
8 o'clock in the evening		wanshang ba dian (wahn-shahng bah dee-in)
What time?	Ji dian?	(Jee dee-in?)
at/in	zai	(zigh)
at noon	zai zhongwu	(zigh joong-wuu)
at four o'clock	zai si dian	(zigh suh dee-in)
at nine o'clock	zai jiu dian	(zigh jew dee-in)
What time is it?	Xianzai jidian?	(Shee-in-zigh jee-dee-in?);
	Jidian zhong?	(Jee-dee-in joong?)
early	zao	(zow)
late	wan	(wahn)
on time	zhunshi	(juwun-shr)
in the morning	zai zaoshang	(zigh zow-shahng)
in the afternoon	zai xiawu	(zigh shee-ah-wuu)
in the evening	zai wanshang	(zigh wahn-shahng)

It is 12 o'clock (noon).
Xianzai zhongwu-le.
(Shee-in-zigh joong-wuu-luh.)

It is one o'clock.
Yi dian.
(Ee dee-in.)

It is two o'clock.
Er dian.
(Urr dee-in.)

It is three o'clock.
San dian.
(Sahn dee-in.)

It is eight o'clock.
Ba dian.
(Bah dee-in.)

It is three o'clock in the afternoon.
Xiawu san dian.
(Shee-ah-wuu sahn dee-in.)

It is one o'clock in the morning.
Shangwu yi dian.
(Shahng-wuu ee dee-in.)

It is 12:30.
Shier dian sanshi.
(Shr-urr dee-in sahn-shr.)

It is 6:30.
Liu dian sanshi.
(Leo dee-in sahn-shr.)

What time are we leaving?
Women shenme shijian zou?
(Waw-mun shuun-muh shr-jee-in zoe?)

What time is your departure?
Ni jidian chufei?
(Nee jee-dee-in chuu-fay?)

What time are we going out?
Women jidian chu qu?
(Waw-mun jee-dee-in chuu chu?)

I have no more time.
Wo meiyou tai duo shijian.
(Waw may-yoe tie dwaw shr-jee-in.)

What time is the appointment?
Yuehui shi jidian?
(Yu-eh-hway shr jee-dee-in?)

What time does the meeting start?
Huiyi jidian kai shi?
(Hway-ee jee-dee-in kigh shr?)

What time shall we get up?
Jidian women qi chuang?
(Jee-dee-in waw-mun chee chwahng?)

What time is the bus leaving?
Jidian gonggong qiche likai?
(Jee-dee-in goong-goong chee-chuh lee-kigh?)

We have plenty of time.
Women you zu gou-de shijian.
(Waw-mun yoe zuu go-duh shr-jee-in.)

What time does breakfast begin?
Zaocan jidian kaishi?
(Zow-tsahn jee-dee-in kigh-shr?)

Breakfast begins at seven o'clock.
Qi zaocan shi jidian.
(Chee zow-tsahn shr jee-dee-in.)

What time is lunch?
Wucan shi jidian?
(Wuu-tsahn shr jee-dee-in?)

Lunch is from noon to one o'clock.
Wucan shi cong shier dian dao yi dian.
(Wuu-tsahn shr tsoong shr-urr dee-in dow ee dee-in.)

What time is dinner?
Wancan shi jidian?
(Wahn-tsahn shr jee-dee-in?)

Dinner is at 7:30.
Wancan shi qidiansanshi.
(Wahn-tsahn shr chee-dee-in-sahn-shr.)

What time do department stores open?
Shangdian jidian kaimen?
(Shahng-dee-in jee-dee-in kigh-mun?)

I'll be back in a short time.
Wo hai hen kuai huilai.
(Waw high hin kwie hway-lie.)

Is it time to go?
Jidian zou?
(Jee-dee-in zoe?)

I'm sorry, my time is up.
Duibuqi, wo shijian dao-le.
(Dway-buu-chee, waw shr-jee-in dow-luh.)

Will this take very much time?
Zhe jiang yong hen chang shijian ma?
(Juh jee-ahng yoong hin chahng shr-jee-in mah?)

Are you free now?
Ni xian zai you shijian ma?
(Nee shee-in zigh yoe shr-jee-in mah?)

When will you be free?
Ni shenme shijian you kong?
(Nee shuun-muh shr-jee-in yoe koong?)

I'll go to Shanghai when I have more time.
Dang wo you shijian wo yao qu Shanghai.
(Dahng waw yoe shr-jee-in waw yow chu Shahng-high.)

We are on time.
Women zhun shi dao.
(Waw-mun juwun shr dow.)

Days

Monday	Xingqiyi	(Sheeng-chee-ee)
Tuesday	Xingqier	(Sheeng-chee-urr)
Wednesday	Xingqisan	(Sheeng-chee-sahn)
Thursday	Xingqisi	(Sheeng-chee-suh)

Friday	Xingqiwu	(Sheeng-chee-wuu)
Saturday	Xingqiliu	(Sheeng-chee-leo)
Sunday	Xingqitian	(Sheeng-chee-tee-in)
day	ri	(rr)
today	jintian	(jeen-tee-in)
tomorrow	mingtian	(meeng-tee-in)
day after tomorrow	houtian	(hoe-tee-in)
yesterday	zuotian	(zwaw-tee-in)
day before yesterday	qiantian	(chee-in-tee-in)
next day	dier tian	(dee-urr tee-in)
day before	qian ti tian	(chee-in tee tee-in)
every day	meitian	(may-tee-in)
during the day	zai baitian	(zigh buy-tee-in)
during the evening	zai wanshang	(zigh wahn-shahng)

Counting days

1 day	yi tian	(ee tee-in)
2 days	er tian	(urr tee-in)
3 days	san tian	(sahn tee-in)
8 days	ba tian	(bah tee-in)
10 days	shi tian	(shr tee-in)
21 days	ershiyi tian	(urr-shr-ee tee-in)
28 days	ershiba tian	(urr-shr-bah tee-in)

How many days are you going to be here?
Ni jiang yong ji tian dao zheli?
(Nee jee-ahng yoong jee tee-in dow juh-lee?)

I/we will be in Shanghai for six days.
Wo jiang zai Shanghai dai liu tian.
(Waw jee-ahng zigh Shahng-high die leo tee-in.)

How many days will it take?
Zhe jiang yong jitian wancheng?
(Juh jee-ahng yoong jee-tee-in wahn-chuung?)

It will take three days.
Zhe jiang yong san tian.
(Juh jee-ahng yoong sahn tee-in.)

What day is today?
Jintian shi xingqi ji?
(Jeen-tee-in shr sheeng-chee jee?)

Today is Monday.
Jintian shi Xingqiyi
(Jeen-tee-in shr Sheeng-chee-ee.)

Tomorrow will be Tuesday.
Mingtian shi Xingqier.
(Meeng-tee-in shr Sheeng-chee-urr.)

Day after tomorrow will be Wednesday.
Huo tian shi Xingqisan.
(Hwaw tee-in shr Sheeng-chee-sahn.)

I will be in Beijing only three days.
Wo jiang zai Beijing dai san tian.
(Waw jee-ahng zigh Bay-jeeng die sahn tee-in.)

Tomorrow I want to meet Mr. Wu.
Mingtian wo yao chu jian Wu Xiansheng.
(Meeng-tee-in waw yow chuu jee-in Wuu
    Shee-in-shuung.)

Please meet me today.
Qing jintian jian wo.
(Cheeng jeen-tee-in jee-in waw.)

Yesterday I ate Peking duck.
Zuotian wo chi de shi Peking ya.
(Zwaw-tee-in waw chee duh shr Peking yah.)

Last night I went to a karaoke bar.
Zuo tian wanshang wo qu-le karaoke jiuba.
(Zwaw tee-in wahn-shahng waw chu-luh kah-rou-kuh
    jeo-bah.)

I really enjoyed yesterday.
Wo zuotian hen gaoxin.
(Waw zwaw-tee-in hin gow-sheen.)

I am going to _____ on Thursday.
Xingqier wo jiang _____.
(Sheeng-chee-urr waw jee-ahng _____.)

I will return to _____ on Friday.
Xingqiwu wo yao huilai gei _____.
(Sheeng-chee-wuu waw yow hway-lie gay _____.)

On Saturday I'm going to meet a friend.
Xingqiliu wo jiang qu jian yi-ge pengyou.
(Sheeng-chee-leo waw jee-ahng chu jee-in ee-guh
   puung-yoe.)

On Sunday I'm going to see a movie.
Xingqiri wo jiang qu kan dian yin.
(Sheeng-chee-rr waw jee-ahng chu kahn dee-in een.)

Weeks

week	xingqi	(sheeng-chee)
this week	zhei-ge xingqi	(jay-guh sheeng-chee)
next week	xia-ge xingqi	(shee-ah-guh sheeng-chee)
last week	shang-ge xingqi	(shahng-guh sheeng-chee)

weekend	zhoumo	(joe-mwo)
week after next	xiaxiage xingqi	(shee-ah-shee-ah-guh sheeng-chee)

When referring to days within the current week, the day is preceded by the word *zhei-ge* (this); when talking about days of the following week, the day is preceded by *shang-ge* (next), and so on.

Will it be ready by next week?
Xia-ge xingqi neng zhun bei hao ma?
(Shee-ah-guh sheeng-chee nuung juwun bay how mah?)

Please wait until the week after next.
Qing deng dao xia xia-ge xingqi.
(Cheeng duung dow shee-ah shee-ah-guh sheeng-chee.)

I will be in Guangzhou until next week.
Wo jiang zai Guangzhou dai dan xia xingqi.
(Waw jee-ahng zigh Gwahng-joe die dahn shee-ah sheeng-chee.)

Altogether, I will be here for three weeks.
Quan jia qilai wo jiang zai zheli dai san-ge xingqi.
(Chwahn jee-ah chee-lie waw jee-ahng zigh juh-lee die sahn-guh sheeng-chee.)

How many weeks have you been in the United States?
Ni jiang zai Meiguo dai ji-ge xingqi?
(Nee jee-ahng zigh May-gwaw die jee-guh sheeng-chee?)

Counting weeks

1 week	yi xingqi	(ee sheeng-chee)
2 weeks	er xingqi liang xingqi	(urr sheeng-chee); (lee-ahng sheeng-chee)
3 weeks	san xingqi	(sahn sheeng-chee)
4 weeks	si xingqi	(suh sheeng-chee)
6 weeks	liu xingqi	(leo sheeng-chee)
7 weeks	qi xingqi	(chee sheeng-chee)
8 weeks	ba xingqi	(bah sheeng-chee)

two weeks ago
liang xingqi yi qian
(lee-ahng sheeng-chee ee chee-in)

two more weeks
liang-ge duo xingqi
(lee-ahng-guh dwaw sheeng-chee)

I will be in China for one week.
Wo jiang zai Zongguo dai yi-ge duo xingqi.
(Waw jee-ahng zigh Joong-gwaw die ee-guh dwaw
sheeng-chee.)

Months

The Chinese word for month is *yue* (yu-eh). The months are numbered instead of named, which makes it a lot easier to remember and use them. Just put the appropriate number before *yue*.

January	Yiyue	(Ee-yu-eh)
February	Eryue	(Urr-yu-eh)
March	Sanyue	(Sahn-yu-eh)
April	Siyue	(Suh-yu-eh)
May	Wuyue	(Wuu-yu-eh)
June	Liuyue	(Leo-yu-eh)
July	Qiyue	(Chee-yu-eh)
August	Bayue	(Bah-yu-eh)
September	Jiuyue	(Jew-yu-eh)
October	Shiyue	(Shr-yu-eh)
November	Shiyiyue	(Shr-ee-yu-eh)
December	Shieryue	(Shr-urr-yu-eh)
this month	zheige yue	(jay-guh yu-eh)
next month	xiage yue	(shee-ah-guh yu-eh)
last month	shangge yue	(shahng-guh yu-eh)
month after next	xiaxiage yue	(shee-ah-shee-ah-guh yu-eh)

| month before last | qiange yue | (chee-in-guh yu-eh) |
| monthly | meige yue | (may-guh yu-eh) |

Counting months

1 month	yi yiyue	(ee ee-yu-eh)
2 months	er yiyue	(urr ee-yu-eh)
3 months	san yiyue	(sahn ee-yu-eh)
4 months	si yiyue	(suh ee-yu-eh)
5 months	wu yiyue	(wuu ee-yu-eh)
6 months	liu yiyue	(leo ee-yu-eh)
7 months	qi yiyue	(chee ee-yu-eh)
8 months	ba yiyue	(bah ee-yu-eh)
9 months	jiu yiyue	(jew ee-yu-eh)
10 months	shi yiyue	(shr ee-yu-eh)
11 months	shiyi yiyue	(shr-ee ee-yu-eh)
12 months	shier yiyue	(shr-urr ee-yu-eh)
a few months	ji-ge yue	(jee-guh yu-eh)
every month	mei-ge yue	(may-guh yu-eh)

How many months have you been here?
Ni yi jin zai zheli ji-ge yue?
(Nee ee jeen zigh juh-lee jee-guh yu-eh?)

I've been in China for five months.
Wo zai Zhongguo wu-ge yue.
(Waw zigh Joong-gwaw wuu-guh yu-eh.)

This project will take two months.
Zhe-ge xiang-liu jiang xue yao liang-ge yue.
(Juh-guh shee-ahng-leo jee-ahng shu-eh yow
    lee-ahng-guh yu-eh.)

My birthday was last month.
Wo-de shengri-le shi shang-ge yue.
(Waw-duh shuung-rr-luh shr shahng-guh yu-eh.)

I will return next month.
Wo xia-ge yue huilai.
(Waw shee-ah-guh yu-eh hway-lie.)

Will it get hot in August?
Bayue jiang hen re ma?
(Bah-yu-eh jee-ahng hin ruh mah?)

I am going to Japan in April.
Siyue wo yao qu Riben.
(Suh-yu-eh waw yow chu Rr-bin.)

Years

year	nian	(nee-in)
this year	jin nian	(jeen nee-in)
last year	qu nian	(chu nee-in)
next year	ming nian	(meeng nee-in)
every year	mei nian	(may nee-in)
all year	quan nian	(chwahn nee-in)
New Year's Day	Yuan Dan	(Ywen Dahn)
Happy New Year	Xin Nian Hao	(Sheen Nee-in How)
for one year	yi nian	(ee nee-in)
for two years	liang nian	(lee-ahng nee-in)
for three years	san nian	(sahn nee-in)
five-and-a-half years	wu nian ban	(wuu nee-in bahn)

I have studied Chinese for one year.
Wo xue Zhongguowen yi nian-le.
(Waw shu-eh Joong-gwaw-wun ee nee-in-luh.)

1996	yijiujiuliu	(ee-jew-jew-leo)
1997	yijiujiuqi	(ee-jew-jew-chee)

1998 yijiujiuba   (ee-jew-jew-bah)

1999 yijiujiujiu   (ee-jew-jew-jew)

2000 lianglinglingling   (lee-ahng-leeng-leeng-leeng)

2001 lianglinglingyi   (lee-ahng-leeng-leeng-ee)

2002 lianglinglingliang (lee-ahng-leeng-leeng-lee-ahng)

2003 lianglinglingsan   (lee-ahng-leeng-leeng-sahn)

2004 lianglinglingsi   (lee-ahng-leeng-leeng-suh)

2005 lianglinglingwu   (lee-ahng-leeng-leeng-wuu)

2010 lianglingyiling   (lee-ahng-leeng-ee-leeng)

He was born in 1980.
Ta chu sheng zai yijiu ba ling nian.
(Tah chuu shuung zigh ee-jew bah leeng nee-in.)

I was born in 1975.
Wo chu sheng zai yijiuqiwu nian.
(Waw chuu shuung zigh ee-jew-chee-wuu nee-in.)

Giving dates

The order of dates in Chinese is the reverse of the English method. Instead of day, month, and year, the Chinese system is year (nian), month (yue), and day (hao).

December 30, 1999
Yijiujiujiu nian shieryue yue sanshi hao
(Ee-jew-jew-jew nee-in, shr-urr-yu-eh yu-eh sahn-shr how)

January 1, 2010
Lianglingyiling nian yiyue yue yi hao
(Lee-ahng-leeng-ee-leeng nee-in, ee-yu-eh yu-eh ee how)

1st (of the month)	yiri*	(ee-rr)
2nd (of the month)	erri	(urr-rr)
3rd (of the month)	sanri	(sahn-rr)
4th (of the month)	siri	(suh-rr)
5th (of the month)	wuri	(wuu-rr)
6th (of the month)	liuri	(leo-rr)
7th (of the month)	qiri	(chi-rr)
8th (of the month)	bari	(bah-rr)
9th (of the month)	jiuri	(jew-rr)
10th (of the month)	shiri	(shr-rr)
11th (of the month)	shiyiri	(shr-ee-rr)
12th (of the month)	shierri	(shr-urr-rr)
15th (of the month)	shiwuri	(shr-wuu-rr)

---

* *Hao* (how) may also be used (in place of *ri*), as in *yihao* (ee-how) and *erhao* (urr-how).

18th (of the month)	shibari	(shr-bah-rr)
20th (of the month)	ershiri	(urr-shr-rr)
21st (of the month)	ershiyiri	(urr-shr-ee-rr)
26th (of the month)	ershiliuri	(urr-shr-leo-rr)
30th (of the month)	sanshiri	(sahn-shr-rr)

We are going to Hong Kong on the twenty-first.
Ershiyi women jiang qu Xiang Guang.
(Urr-shr-ee waw-mun jee-ahng chu Shee-ahng Gwahng.)

Tomorrow will be the sixth.
Mingtian shiliuhao.
(Meeng-tee-in shr-leo-how.)

We leave on the eighteenth.
Women shibari likai.
(Waw-mun shr-bah-rr lee-kigh.)

Please respond/reply by July 15th.
Qing qiyue shiwuri huida.
(Cheeng chee-yu-eh shr-wuu-rr hway-dah.)

Today is the 28th of November.
Jintian shi shiyiyue ershibari.
(Jeen-tee-in shr shr-ee-yu-eh urr-shr-bah-rr.)

Money Matters

Renminbi, which literally means "people's money," is the official designation for China's currency. The Chinese

111

equivalent of the word "dollar" (the currency denomination) is *yuan* (ywen). There is also an old colloquial term, *kuai* (kwye), which is commonly used instead of *yuan*. *Kuai*, which literally means "lump" or "piece," came into use a long time ago when money consisted of lumps of melted metal. The *yuan* (or Chinese "dollar") is made up of 100 *fen* (fun), and 10 *mao* (mou). *Mao* are commonly called *jiao* (jee-ow). The currency comes in denominations of 1-, 5-, 10-, and 50-*yuan* notes. There are also 1-, 2- and 5-*fen* coins.

Foreign Exchange Certificates are a special currency designed for use by foreigners in China. They come in the same demominations as the *yuan*, and are popularly known as FECs.

money	qian	(chee-in)
cash	xiankuan xianjin	(shee-in-kwahn); (shee-in-jeen)
Chinese currency	renminbi	(wren-meen-bee)
1 yuan	yi yuan yi kuai	(ee ywen); (ee kwie)
2 yuan	liang yuan liang kuai	(lee-ahng ywen); (lee-ahng kwie)
5 yuan	wu yuan wu kuai	(wuu ywen); (wuu kwie)
10 yuan	shi yuan shi kuai	(shr ywen); (shr kwie)

5 jiao	wu jiao wu mao	(wuu jee-ow); (wuu mou)
Foreign Exchange Certificates	Wai Hui Juan	(wigh hway jwen)
bill (currency note)	chaopiao	(chow-pee-ow)
credit card	xinyong ka	(sheen-yoong kah)
traveler's checks	luxing zhipiao	(luu-sheeng jr-pee-ow)
U.S. dollars	Mei yuan	(may ywen)
Hong Kong dollars	Gang bi	(Gahng bee)
Japanese yen	Ri yuan	(Rr ywen)
Australian dollars	Aodaliya yuan Aobi	(Ah-aw-dah-lee- yah ywen); (Ah-aw-bee)
Canadian dollars	Jiabi	(Jee-ah-bee)
English pounds	Ying bang	(Eeng bahng)
French francs	Fa lang	(Fah lahng)
German marks	Xide make	(She-duh mah-kuh)

Italian lira	Yidali lila	(Ee-dah-lee lee-lah)
exchange rate	diuhuan lu	(deo-hwahn luu)
exchange money	diuhuan qian	(deo-hwahn chee-in)
small change	ling qian	(leeng chee-in)
small bills	xiao chaopiao	(shee-ow chow-pee-ow)
large bills	da chaopiao	(dah chow-pee-ow)
cashier's check	yinghang benpiao	(eeng-hahng bin-pee-ow)
endorse (check)	beishu	(bay-shuu)
money order	huikuan dan	(hway-kwahn dahn)
signature	qianming	(chee-in-meeng)

Where can I exchange money?
Nali keyi duihuan qian?
(Nah-lee kuh-ee dway-hwahn chee-in?)

Where is the bank?
Yin hang zai nar?
(Een hahng zigh nah-urr?)

What is today's exchange rate for U.S. dollars?
Jintian Mei yuan duihuan lu duoshao?
(Jeen-tee-in May ywen dway-hwahn luu dwaw-shou?)

How much is that in U.S. dollars?
Zhe zhi duoshao Mei yuan?
(Juh jr dwaw-shou May ywen?)

Please give me (some) small bills.
Qing gei wo xiao chaopiao.
(Cheeng gay waw shee-ow chow-pee-ow.)

Please give me (some) small change.
Qing gei wo ling qian.
(Cheeng gay waw leeng chee-in.)

I would like to change traveler's checks.
Wo xiang duihuan dianr qian.
(Waw shee-ahng dway-hwahn dee-in-urr chee-in.)

I forgot my money.
Wo wang-le wo-de qian.
(Waw wahng-luh waw-duh chee-in.)

Can you cash a personal check?
Keyi duihuan siren zhipiao ma?
(Kuh-ee dway-hwahn suh-wren jr-pee-ow mah?)

Please loan me 5,000 yuan.
Qing Jie gei wo wuqian yuan.
(Cheeng jee-eh gay waw wuu-chee-in ywen.)

115

Immigration and Customs

arrivals	jinguan	(jeen-gwahn)
departures	chuguan	(chuu-gwahn)
documents	wenjian	(wun-jee-in)
immigration	yimin jiancha zhan	(ee-meen jee-in-chah jahn)
passport	huzhao	(huu-jow)
health card	zhengming shu	(juung-meeng shuu)
visa	qianzheng	(chee-in-juung)
baggage	xingli	(sheeng-lee)
baggage cart	xingli che	(sheeng-lee chuh)
baggage claim	xingli ting	(sheeng-lee teeng)
baggage tag	xingli pai	(sheeng-lee pie)
customs	haiguan	(high-gwahn)
declaration form	shenbao dan	(shuun-bow dahn)

inspection	jiancha	(jee-in-chah)
customs duties	guanshui	(gwahn-shway)
duty free	mianshui	(mee-in-shway)
contraband	zousi	(zoe-suh)
antiques	gudong	(guu-doong)
drugs	dupin	(duu-peen)
exchange counter	duihuan chu	(dway-hwahn chuu)
exchange rate	duihuan lu	(dway-hwahn luu)
porter	fuyuyuan	(fuu-yuu-ywen)
on business	zuo shengyi	(zwaw shuung-ee)
on vacation	zuo dujia	(zwaw duu-jee-ah)
tour	youlan luxing	(yoe-lahn); (luu-sheeng)
on tour	zuo luxing	(zwaw luu-sheeng)
tour group	luyou tuan	(luu-yoe twahn)

husband	zhangfu	(jahng-fuu)
wife	taitai	(tie-tie)
family	jiaren	(jee-ah-wren)
gifts	lipin	(lee-peen)
samples	yangpin	(yahng-peen)
personal use	ziji yong-de	(dzu-jee yoong-duh)

My name is _____.
Wo-de mingzi shi _____.
(Waw-duh meeng-dzu shr _____.)

I am an American.
Wo shi Meiguoren.
(Waw shr May-gwaw-wren.)

I'm here on vacation.
Wo lai dujia.
(Waw lie duu-jee-ah.)

I'll be staying at the Lido Holiday Inn.
Wo hui zhu zai Lido Holiday Inn.
(Waw hway juu zigh Lee-doh Holiday Inn.)

I am traveling by myself.
Wo dandu luxing.
(Waw dahn-duu luu-sheeng.)

I'm traveling on business.
Wo zuo shengyi luxing.
(Waw zwaw shuung-ee luu-sheeng.)

I'm traveling with friends.
Wo gen wo-de pengyou luxing.
(Waw gun waw-duh puung-yoe luu-sheeng.)

I have nothing to declare.
Wo meiyou yao baoguan-de dongxi.
(Waw may-yoe yow bow-gwahn-duh doong-she.)

I will be here for about two weeks.
Wo yao zhu er-ge xingqi.
(Waw yow juu urr-guh sheeng-chee.)

Have you finished your inspection?
Jiancha wan-le ma?
(Jee-in-chah wahn-luh mah?)

Transportation
Airplane travel

airport	feijichang	(fay-jee-chahng)
airplane	feiji	(fay-jee)
airline	hangkong gongsi	(hahng-koong goong-suh)
flight	hangban	(hahng-bahn)
flight number	hangban haoma	(hahng-bahn how-mah)
reservations	yuding	(yuu-deeng)

first class	toudeng-cang	(toe-duung tsahng)
first-class ticket	toudeng piao	(toe-duung pee-ow)
economy class	jingji cang	(jeeng-jee tsahng)
economy-class ticket	putong piao	(puu-toong pee-ow)
cancel	quxiao	(chu-shee-ow)
confirm	queren	(chu-uh-wren)
arrival time	rugang shijian	(ruu-gahng shr-jee-in)
arrival gate	rugang rukou	(ruu-gahng ruu-koe)
connecting flight	xianjie hangban	(shee-in-jee-eh hahng-bahn)
check in (airport)	ban chengji shouxu	(bahn chuung-jee show-shu)
check-in counter	jianpiao chu	(jee-in pee-ow chuu)
check-in time	jianpiao shijian	(jee-in-pee-ow shr-jee-in)

departure tax	jichang fei	(jee-chahng fay)
departure time	qifei shijian	(chee-fay shr-jee-in)
boarding card or pass	dengji ka	(duung-jee kah)
boarding aircraft	shang feiji	(shahng fay-jee)
departing aircraft	xia feiji	(shee-ah fay-jee)
departing gate	xia rukou	(shee-ah ruu-koe)
departure lounge	houji ting	(hoe-jee teeng)
departure time	chugang shijian	(chuu-gahng shr-jee-in)
carry-on baggage	shouti-bao	(show-tee-bow)
seat	zuowei	(zwaw-way)
aisle seat	kaozao dao zuowei	(kow-zow dow zwaw-way)
window seat	kaochuang zuowei	(kow-chwahng zwaw-way)
seat belt	anquan dai	(ahn-chwahn die)

smoking section	neng chouyan	(nuung choe-yahn)
nonsmoking section	bu xu chouyan	(buu shu choe-yahn)
take off	qifei	(chee-fay)
landing	jiangluo	(jee-ahng-lwaw)
waiting room	houche shi	(hoe-chuh shr)
passport	huzhao	(huu-jow)
passport control	jianyan huzhao	(jee-in-yahn huu-jow)
health certificate	jiankang zhengming	(jee-in-kahng juung-meeng)
customs	haiguan	(high-gwahn)
customs duties	guanshui	(gwahn-shway)
duty free	mianshui	(mee-in-shway)
customs form	shenbao dan	(shuun-bow dahn)
baggage claim	xingli fang	(sheeng-lee fahng)
claim check	xingli piao	(sheeng-lee pee-ow)

taxi stand	chuzu qiche zhan	(chuu-zuu chee-chuh jahn)
airport shuttle bus	jichang jie songche	(jee-chahng jee-eh soong-chuh)
hotel shuttle bus	luguan jie songche	(luu-gwahn jee-eh soong-chuh)

The airport, please.
Qing qu jichang.
(Cheeng chu jee-chahng.)

Japan Airlines, please.
Riben Hangkong Gongsi.
(Rr-bin Hahng-koong Goong-suh.)

What time does the plane take off?
Feiji shenme shihou qifei?
(Fay-jee shuun-muh shr-hoe chee-fay?)

How long does it take to get to the airport?
Dao jichang yao duoshao shijian?
(Dow jee-chahng yow dwaw-shou shr-jee-in?)

Train travel

In the Chinese system, first-class accommodations on trains and ships are generally referred to as "soft" (class), whereas second- or third-class accommodations are called "hard" (class).

Chinese National Railways	Zhongguo Tielu	(Joong-gwaw Tee-eh-luu)
train	huoche	(hwaw-chuh)
train station	huoche zhan	(hwaw-chuh jahn)
express train	kuai che	(kwie chuh)
local train	putong che	(puu-toong chuh)
slow train	man che	(mahn chuh)
ticket	piao	(pee-ow)
ticket office	shou piao chu	(show pee-ow chuu)
ticket seller	shou piao yuan	(show pee-ow ywen)
adult ticket	daren piao	(dah-wren pee-ow)
child ticket	ertong piao	(urr-toong pee-ow)
one-way ticket	dan cheng piao	(dahn chuung pee-ow)
round-trip ticket	laihui piao	(lie-hway pee-ow)

first-class ticket	tou-deng piao	(toe-duung pee-ow)
economy-class ticket	putong piao	(puu-toong pee-ow)
soft-class (ticket)	ruan wo pu	(rwahn waw puu)
hard-class (ticket)	ying wo pu	(eeng waw puu)
soft seat	ruan zuo	(rwahn zwaw)
soft sleeper	ruan wo	(rwahn waw)
hard seat	ying zuo	(eeng zwaw)
hard sleeper	ying wo	(eeng waw)
compartment	chexiang	(chuh-shee-ahng)
seat	weizi	(way-dzu)
reserved seat ticket	yuding zuowei piao	(yuu-deeng zwaw-way pee-ow)
unreserved seat ticket	wu yuding zuowei piao	(wuu yuu-deeng zwaw-way pee-ow)
boarding platform	yuetai	(yu-eh-tie)

platform ticket	zhantai piao	(jahn-tie pee-ow)
departure time	kai jidian	(kigh jee-dee-in)
arrival time	dao jidian	(dow jee-dee-in)
dining car	can che	(tsahn chuh)
transfer	dao huan	(dow); (hwahn)
disembark, get off	xia shangan	(shee-ah); (shahng-ahn)
board, get on	shang che	(shahng-chuh)
stop	ting	(teeng)
entrance	rukou	(ruu-koe)
exit (noun)	chukou	(chuu-koe)
exit (verb)	tuichu	(tway-chuu)

Where is the train station?
Che zhen zai nali?
(Chuh jun zigh nah-lee?)

Where is the ticket office?
Nali shi shou piao chu?
(Nah-lee shr show pee-ow chuu?)

I want to go to _____.
Wo yao qu _____.
(Waw yow chu _____.)

What is the track number?
Ji hao huoche?
(Jee how hwaw-chuh?)

What is the platform number for Shanghai?
Qu Shanghai zai ji hao tai?
(Chu Shahng-high zigh jee how tie?)

How much is it to Guangzhou?
Qu Guangzhou duoshao qian?
(Chu Gwahng-joe dwaw-shou chee-in?)

Do I have to transfer anywhere?
Wo jiang zai rali huache?
(Waw jee-ahng zigh rah-lee hwah-chuh?)

Excuse me, is this the train for Shanghai?
Duibuqi, zhe lie huoche shi qu Shanghai-de ma?
(Dway-buu-chee, juh lee-eh hwaw-chuh shr chu
    Shahng-high-duh mah?)

Where are we now?
Women xianzai zai nar?
(Waw-mun shee-in-zigh zigh nahr?)

I want to upgrade my ticket.
Wo xiang bu piao.
(Waw shee-ahng buu pee-ow.)

Travel by ship

steamer, boat	lunchuan	(lwun-chwahn)
ship ticket	chuan piao	(chwahn pee-ow)

cabin	cang	(tsahng)
stateroom	tedeng cang	(tuh-duung tsahng)
first-class cabin	toudeng cang	(toe-duung tsahng)
second-class cabin	erdeng cang	(urr-duung tsahng)
third-class cabin	sandeng cang	(sahn-duung tsahng)
fourth-class cabin	sideng cang	(suh-duung tsahng)
passenger office	keyun shi	(kuh-ywun shr)
service counter	fuwu bu	(fuu-wuu buu)
snack counter	xiaomai bu	(shee-ow-my buu)
deck	jiaban	(jee-ah-bahn)
captain (of ship)	chuanzhang	(chwahn-jahng)
pilot's bridge	jiashi tai	(jee-ah-shr tie)
harbor, port	gangkou	(gahng-koe)
dock (noun)	matou	(mah-toe)

sail (depart)	hangxing	(hahng-sheeng)
sailing schedule	chuanqi biao	(chwahn-chee bee-ow)
leave port	chu gang	(chuu gahng)
enter port	jin gang	(jeen gahng)
go ashore	kao an	(kow ahn)

I want to go by ship.
Wo xiang zuo chuan qu.
(Waw shee-ahng zwaw chwahn chu.)

What time can I board the ship?
Jidian wo keyi shang chuan?
(Jee-dee-in waw kuh-ee shahng chwahn?)

What time does the ship sail?
Chuan jidian kai?
(Chwahn jee-dee-in kigh?)

How big is the ship?
Chuan you duo da?
(Chwahn yoe dwaw dah?)

I want to buy (some) seasick pills.
(Wo yao mai yunchuan-de yaowan.)
(Waw yow my ywun-chwahn-duh yow-wahn.)

Subways

subway	dixiatielu	(dee-shee-ah-tee-eh-luu)

subway station   dixiatielu zhan   (dee-shee-ah-tee-
eh-luu jahn)

Can we go by subway?
Women neng yong dixiatie qu ma?
(Waw-mun nuung yoong dee-shee-ah-tee-eh chu mah?)

Let's go by subway.
Women zuo dixiatie qu.
(Waw-mun zwaw dee-she-ah-tee-eh chu.)

Where is the nearest subway station?
Zuijin di dixiatie chezhan zai nali?
(Zway-jeen dee dee-she-ah-tee-eh chuh-jahn zigh
nah-lee?)

How much does it cost?
Duoshao jiaqian?
(Dwaw-shou jee-ah-chee-in?)

Taxis

taxi   chuzuqiche   (chuu-zuu-chee-chuh)

taxi stand   chuzuqiche zhan   (chuu-zuu-chee-chuh
jahn)

driver   siji   (suh-jee)

fare   piaojia   (pee-ow-jee-ah)

kilometer   gongli   (goong-lee)

Please call a taxi for me.
Qing gei wo jiao che.
(Cheeng gay waw jee-ow chuh.)

Do you speak English?
Ni hui jiang Yingyu ma?
(Nee hway jee-ahng Eeng-yuu mah?)

I want to go to _____.
Wo yao qu _____.
(Waw yow chu _____.)

Please take me to _____.
Qing song wo dao _____.
(Cheeng soong waw dow _____.)

Please take me to this address.
Qing dai wo dao zheige dizhi.
(Cheeng die waw dow jay-guh dee-jr.)

Do you know where it is?
Ni zhidao zai nali ma?
(Nee jr-dow zigh nah-lee mah?)

How far (is it)?
You duo yuan?
(Yoe dwaw ywen?)

How long (will it take)?
Duo jiu?
(Dwaw jeo?)

How much is it to _____?
Qu _____ duoshao qian?
(Chu _____ dwaw-shou chee-in?)

That's too much (expensive)!
Tai gui-le!
(Tie gway-luh!)

How many kilometers is it?
You duo shao gongli?
(Yoe dwaw shou goong-lee?)

Please go to Tiananmen Square.
Qing qu Tiananmen Guang Cheng.
(Cheeng chu Tee-in Ahn Mun Gwahng Chuung.)

Do you know the _____ hotel?
Ni zhidao _____ luguan ma?
(Nee jr-dow _____ luu-gwahn mah?)

I'm in a hurry.
Wo hen zhao ji.
(Waw hin jow jee.)

How many minutes will it take?
Xu yao duo shao shijian?
(Shu yow dwaw shou shr-jee-in?)

Please turn left.
Qing xiang zuo zuan.
(Cheeng shee-ahng zwaw zwahn.)

Please turn right.
Qing xiang you zuan
(Cheeng shee-ahng yoe zwahn.)

Please go straight.
Qing xiang qian.
(Cheeng shee-ahng chee-in.)

Please stop here.
Qing zai zheli ting.
(Cheeng zigh juh-lee teeng.)

Please stop near the intersection.
Qing ting zai shizilukou fujin.
(Cheeng teeng zigh shr-dzu-luu-koe fuu-jeen.)

Please stop at the next corner.
Qing zai guai wanchu ting.
(Cheeng zigh gwie wahn-chuu teeng.)

Can you wait for me?
Ni neng deng wo ma?
(Nee nuung duung waw mah?)

Please wait (for me).
Qing ni deng yi deng.
(Cheeng nee duung ee duung.)

Please take me back to the hotel.
Qing song wo hui luguan.
(Cheeng soong waw hway luu-gwahn.)

Bicycling

bicycle   zixingche   (dzu-sheeng-chuh)

I would like to rent a bicycle.
Wo xiang zu yi-liang zixingche.
(Waw shee-ahng zuu ee-lee-ahng dzu-sheeng-chuh.)

Where can I rent a bicycle?
Wo zai nar keyi zu zixingche?
(Waw zigh nah-urr kuh-ee zuu dzu-sheeng-chuh?)

How much by the hour?
Duoshao qian yi xiao shi?
(Dwaw-shou chee-in ee shee-ow shr?)

How much by the day?
Yitian duoshao qian?
(Ee-tee-in dwaw-shou chee-in?)

How much is the deposit?
Yajin yao duoshao?
(Yah-jeen yow dwaw-shou?)

Hotel Matters

There are several words for "hotel" in Chinese, each with a slightly different connotation, depending on its origin. Older establishments are more likely to use one of the traditional terms that refer to "place for eating" or "place for drinking." The most common of the designations are as follows:

place for guests (guest house)	binguan	(bin-gwahn)
place for eating	fandian	(fahn-dee-in)
place for travelers	luguan ludian	(luu-gwahn); (luu-dee-in)
place for liquor	jiudian	(jeo-dee-in)
place for entertaining *or* guest house	zhaodaisuo	(jow-die-swaw)

Originally, *binguan* and *fandian* referred primarily to luxury-class hotels, and *luguan* to first-class or ordinary hotels, but *luguan* is now commonly used as a generic term for hotel.

When saying room numbers in Chinese, each digit is sounded out. Room 808 is *ba ling ba* (bah leeng bah); not eight hundred and eight.

As of this writing, China still maintains a split-level pricing policy on many products and services, based on nationality and other factors. Foreigners are generally charged substantially higher prices than Chinese. Overseas Chinese are in a special category and are charged less than other foreigners. All students who have student identification get special discounts.

China has a 220-volt, 50-cycle electrical system, so appliances made in the United States for the American market do not work well or at all without a voltage adaptor (which some hotels supply for guests). In addition, most electrical outlets in China are three-pronged with a configuration that is different from American outlets. Some visitors carry outlet adaptors with them. If you are going to remain in China for a lengthy period, it is best to prepare in advance by taking appliances with built-in voltage conversion switches.

vacancy (room)	fangjian	(fahng-jee-in)
reservations	yuding	(yuu-deeng)
check in, register	dengji	(duung-jee)
check out (verb)	tuifang	(tway-fahng)
registration desk	dengji tai	(duung-jee tie)
lobby	qianting	(chee-in-teeng)
one night	yi ye	(ee yeh)

two nights	liang ye	(lee-ahng yeh)
three nights	san ye	(sahn yeh)
four nights	si ye	(suh yeh)
service (bell) desk	fuwu tai	(fuu-wuu tie)
cashier	chunayuan	(chwun-ah-ywen)
key	yaoshi	(yow shr)
room	fangjian	(fahng-jee-in)
room number	fangjian haoma	(fahng-jee-in how-mah)
room rate	fang fei	(fahng fay)
service charge	fuwu fei	(fuu-wuu fay)
single room	danjian	(dahn-jee-in)
double room	shuangren fang	(shwahng-wren fahng)
suite	taojian	(tou-jee-in)
bed	chuang	(chwahng)
twin bed	danren chuang	(dahn-wren chwahng)

bath	xizao	(she-zow)
floor	ceng	(tsuung)
elevator	dianti	(dee-in-tee)
stairs	louti	(low-tee)
floor monitor	fuwu yuan	(fuu-wuu ywen)
housekeeping	kefang bu	(kuh-fahng buu)
refrigerator	bingxiang	(beeng-shee-ahng)
television	dianshi	(dee-in-shr)
radio	shouyinji	(show-een-jee)
air conditioning	kongtiao lengqi	(koong-tee-ow); (luung-chee)
electric fan	dian shan	(dee-in shahn)
heating	nuanqi	(nwahn-chee)
blanket	chuang tanzi	(chwahng tahn-dzu)
sheets	chuangdan	(chwahng-dahn)

pillow	zhentou	(jun-toe)
hangers	yijia	(ee-jee-ah)
clean	ganjing	(gahn-jeeng)
not clean	bu ganjing	(buu gahn-jeeng)
bar of soap	kuai feizao	(kwie fay-zow)
towel	maojin	(mou-jeen)
water	shui	(shway)
boiled drinking water	leng kai shui	(luung kigh shway)
hot water	re shui	(ruh shway)
ice cubes	bing kuai	(beeng kwie)
drinking glasses	boli bei	(bwo-lee bay)
toilet paper	weisheng zhi	(way-shuung jr)
laundry	xiyidian	(she-ee-dee-in)
dry-cleaning	ganxi	(gahn-she)
voltage	dianya	(dee-in-yah)
coffee shop	kafei dian	(kah-fay dee-in)

dining room	can ting	(tsahn teeng)
drugstore	yaodian	(yow-dee-in)
barber shop	lifa dian	(lee-fah dee-in)
haircut	lifa	(lee-fah)
shave	gualian	(gwah-lee-in)
beauty parlor	lifa dian	(lee-fah dee-in)
business center	shangwu zhongxin	(shahng-wuu joong-sheen)
English newspaper	Yingwen baozhi	(Eeng-wun bow-jr)
post office	you ju	(yoe juu)
shopping arcade	gou wu shangchang	(go wuu shahng-chahng)
message	xinxi	(sheen-she)
wake-up call	jiaoxing dianhua	(jee-ow-sheeng dee-in-hwah)
emergency exit	jizhen chukou	(jee-jun chuu-koe)
in-house phone	nei xian (dianhua)	(nay shee-in dee-in-hwah)

My name is De Mente.
Wo-de mingzi shi De Mente.
(Waw-duh meeng-dzu shr De Mente.)

I have a reservation.
Wo yuding le fangjian.
(Waw yuu-deeng luh fahng-jee-in.)

I don't have a reservation.
Wo mei you yuding.
(Waw may yoe yuu-deeng.)

What is my room number?
Wo-de fangjian shi ji hao?
(Waw-duh fahng-jee-in shr jee how?)

How much is the room rate?
Fang fei duoshao qian?
(Fahng fay dwaw-shou chee-in?)

What time is check out?
Shenme shijian tuimang
(Shuun-muh shr-jee-in tway-mahng?)

What time does the coffee shop open?
Kafei dian jidian kaimen?
(Kah-fay dee-in jee-dee-in kigh-mun?)

Where is the coffee shop?
Kafei dian zai nali?
(Kah-fay dee-in zigh nah-lee?)

Where is the dining room?
Can ting zai nali?
(Tsahn teeng zigh nah-lee?)

Please clean my room.
Qing dasao wo-de fangjian.
(Cheeng dah-sow waw-duh fahng-jee-in.)

I would like another blanket, please.
Wo xihuan liuyi-ge maotan.
(Waw she-hwahn leo-ee-guh mou-tahn.)

Are there any messages for me?
Zheli you wo-de liuyan ma?
(Juh-lee yoe waw-duh leo-yahn mah?)

Can you extend my reservations?
Ni neng yan cheng wo-de yuyue ma?
(Nee nuung yahn chuung waw-duh yuu-yu-eh mah?)

I would like to stay for three more days.
Wo yuan yi dai san tian yi shang.
(Waw ywen ee die sahn tee-in ee shahng.)

Where is your business service center?
Nali shi shangwu fuwu zhongxin?
(Nah-lee shr shahng-wuu fuu-wuu joong-sheen?)

Do you have secretarial service?
Ni you mishu fuwu ma?
(Nee yoe me-shuu fuu-wuu mah?)

Do you have a map of the city?
Ni you cheng shi ditu ma?
(Nee yoe chuung shr dee-tuu mah?)

Can you recommend a Chinese restaurant?
Ni neng tui jian yi-ge Zhongguo can guan ma?
(Nee nuung tway jee-in ee-guh Joong-gwaw tsahn
    gwahn mah?)

141

How far is it from the hotel?
Li luguan you duo yuan?
(Lee luu-gwahn yoe dwaw ywen?)

Is there a pharmacy near the hotel?
Luguan fujin you yaodian ma?
(Luu-gwahn fuu-jeen yoe yow-dee-in mah?)

Can I walk there from the hotel?
Wo neng cong luguan zao qu ma?
(Waw nuung tsoong luu-gwahn zow chu mah?)

Please call me a taxi.
Qing bang wo jiao yi liang chuzuche.
(Cheeng bahng waw jee-ow ee lee-ahng chuu-zuu-chuh.)

Introductions

introduce, introduction	jieshao	(jee-eh-shou)
family name	xing	(sheeng)
given name	mingzi	(meeng-dzu)
family and given name	xingming	(sheeng-meeng)
name-card	ming zi	(meeng dzu)
friend	pengyou	(puung-yoe)

boyfriend   nan pengyou   (nahn puung-
                                        yoe)

girlfriend   nu pengyou   (nuu puung-yoe)

May I introduce myself?
Wo keyi jieshao woziji ma?
(Waw kuh-ee jee-eh-shou waw-dzu-jee mah?)

My name is De Mente.
Wo-de mingzi shi De Mente.
(Waw-duh meeng-dzu shr De Mente.)

What is your name?
Ni jiao shenme mingzi?
(Nee jee-ow shuun-muh meeng-dzu?)

What is his/her name?
Ta jiao shenme mingzi?
(Tah jee-ow shuun-muh meeng-dzu?)

Please introduce me to that man.
Qing jiang wo jieshao gai zhewei xiansheng.
(Cheeng jee-ahng waw jee-eh-shou guy juh-way
   shee-in-shuung.)

I would like to introduce Mr. Lee.
Wo jiang wo jieshao Lee Xiansheng.
(Waw jee-ahng waw jee-eh-shou Lee Shee-in-shuung.)

I'm pleased to meet you.
Jiuyang.
(Jew-yahng.)

This is Mr. Adams.
Zhe shi Adams Xiansheng.
(Juh shr Adams Shee-in-shuung.)

Here is my name-card.
Zhe shi wo-de mingpian.
(Juh shr waw-duh meeng-pee-in.)

May I have one of your cards?
Wo keyi na yizheng mingpian ma?
(Waw kuh-ee nah ee-juung meeng-pee-in mah?)

Family members

children	haizi	(high-dzu)
daughter	nuer	(nuu-urr)
son	erzi	(urr-dzu)
parents	fumu	(fuu-muu)
father	baba	(bah-bah)
mother	muqin mama	(muu-cheen); (mah-mah)
husband	zhangfu	(jahng-fuu)
wife	taitai qizi	(tie-tie); (chee-dzu)
older brother	gege	(guh-guh)
younger brother	didi	(dee-dee)

144

older sister	jiejie	(jee-eh-jee-eh)
younger sister	meimei	(may-may)
grandparents	zufumu	(zuu-fuu-muu)
grandchildren	sunci	(suun-tsu)
grandfather (maternal)	laoye	(lou-yeh)
grandfather (paternal)	yeye	(yeh-yeh)
grandmother (maternal)	laolao	(lou-lou)
grandmother (paternal)	nainai	(nigh-nigh)
granddaughter (son's)	sunnu	(suun-nuu)
granddaughter (daughter's)	waisunnu	(wigh-suun-nuu)
grandson (son's)	sunzi	(suun-dzu)
grandson (daughter's)	waisunzi	(wigh-suun-dzu)
marry, married	jiehun	(jee-eh-hwun)

Are you married?
Ni jiehun le ma?
(Nee jee-eh-hwun luh mah?)

Do you have children?
Ni you xiaohai ma?
(Nee yoe shee-ow-high mah?)

I have two daughters.
Wo you liang ge nuer.
(Waw yoe lee-ahng guh nuu-urr.)

I have a son.
Wo you ge erzi.
(Waw yoe guh urr-dzu.)

How is your husband?
Ni zheng fu hao ma?
(Nee juung fuu how mah?)

How is your wife?
Ni taitai hao ma?
(Nee tie-tie how mah?)

She/he is well, thank you.
Ta hen hao, xiexie.
(Tah hin how, she-eh-she-eh.)

I'm quite well, thank you.
Wo hen hao, xiexie.
(Waw hin how, she-eh-she-eh.)

Please tell your wife I said hello.
Qing dai wo wenyi taitai hao.
(Cheeng die waw wun-ee tie-tie how.)

Please give my regards to your father.
Qing dai wo xiang yi fu qin wen hao.
(Cheeng die waw shee-ahng ee fuu cheen wun how.)

How old are you? (to young children)
Ni ji sui?
(Nee jee sway?)

How old are you? (to all others)
Ni duo da?
(Nee dwaw dah?)

Seasons and Weather
Seasons   Jijie (Jee-jee-eh)

spring	chunji	(chwun-jee)
springtime	zai chuntian	(zigh chwun-tee-in)
summer	xiaji	(shee-ah-jee)
summertime	zai xiatian	(zigh shee-ah-tee-in)
fall	qiuji	(cheo-jee)
autumn	qiutian	(cheo-tee-in)
winter	dongji	(doong-jee)

When does spring begin in Beijing?
Zai Beijing chuntian shenme shihou kaishi?
(Zigh Bay-jeeng chwun-tee-in shuun-muh shr-hoe
    kigh-shr?)

Is Beijing hot during the summertime?
Beijing-de xiatian re ma?
(Bay-jeeng-duh shee-ah-tee-in ruh mah?)

What is the best season in Beijing?
Beijing-de nayi-ge jijie zuihao?
(Bay-jeeng-duh nah-ee-guh jee-jee-eh zway-how?)

What is the best season in Shanghai?
Shanghai-de nayi-ge jijie zuihao?
(Shahng-high-duh nah-ee-guh jee-jee-eh zway-how?)

Does it get cold in Guangzhou in winter?
Guangzhou dongtian leng ma?
(Gwahng-joe doong-tee-in luung mah?)

When is the most popular wedding season?
Shenme shihou jiehun de ren zuiduo?
(Shuun-muh shr-hoe jee-eh-hwun duh wren zway-dwaw?)

When does the winter season start in Beijing?
Beijing-de dongtian shenme shihou kaishi?
(Bay-jeeng-duh doong-tee-in shuun-muh shr-hoe
   kigh-shr?)

Weather   Tianqi (Tee-in-chee)

weather forecast	tianqi yubao	(tee-in-chee yuu-bow)
hot	re	(ruh)
cold	leng	(luung)

temperature	qiwen	(chee-wun)
Fahrenheit	huashi wenduji de	(hwah-shr wun-duu-jee duh)
centigrade	sheshi wenduji de	(shuh-shr wun-duu-jee duh)
cloudy	tianyin	(tee-in-een)
windy	guafeng-de	(gwah-fuung-duh)
rain	yushui	(yuu-shway)
raining	xiayu	(shah-yuu)
storm	baofengyu	(bow-fuung-yuu)
heavy rain	da yu	(dah yuu)
typhoon	taifeng	(tie-fuung)
snow	xue	(shu-eh)
snowing	xiaxue	(shee-ah-shu-eh)
dust	chentu	(chuun-tuu)
humidity	shiqi	(shr-chee)
humid, damp	chaoshi menre	(chow-shr); (mun-ruh)

good weather	hao tianqi	(how tee-in-chee)
bad weather	bu hao tianqi	(buu how tee-in-chee)
raincoat	yuyi	(yuu-ee)
umbrella	yusan	(yuu-sahn)

It's hot.
Man re du.
(Mahn ruh duu.)

It's cold.
Man leng de.
(Mahn luung duh.)

It's cold today.
Jintian man leng de.
(Jeen-tee-in mahn luung duh.)

It's raining.
Xia yu le.
(Shee-ah yuu luh.)

It's snowing.
Xia xue le.
(Shee-ah shu-eh luh.)

It's windy.
Feng da.
(Fuung dah.)

It's sunny.
You taiyang.
(Yoe tie-yahng.)

What is the weather forecast for tomorrow?
Mingtian de tianqi yubao shi shenme?
(Meeng-tee-in duh tee-in-chee yuu-bow shr shuun-muh?)

Will it rain tonight?
Jintian wanshang xia yu ma?
(Jeen-tee-in wahn-shahng shee-ah yuu mah?)

It looks like it will rain today.
Jintian kan qi lai yao xia yu.
(Jeen-tee-in kahn chee lie yow shee-ah yuu.)

It should clear up by this afternoon.
Jintian xia wu tianqi bian qing.
(Jeen-tee-in shee-ah wuu tee-in-chee bee-in cheeng.)

The weather is beautiful.
Tianqi hao jile.
(Tee-in-chee how jee-luh.)

How much snow does Beijing have in winter?
Zai Beijing dongtian xia duoshao xue?
(Zigh Bay-jeeng doong-tee-in shee-ah dwaw-shou
    shu-eh?)

Does it snow in Guangzhou?
Guangzhou xia xue ma?
(Gwahngjoe shee-ah shu-eh mah?)

When is the rainy season in Beijing?
Beijing-de yu ji shenme shihou kaishi?
(Bay-jeeng-duh yuu jee shuun-muh shr-hoe kigh-shr?)

Does Shanghai have a rainy season?
Shanghai you yu ji ma?
(Shahng-high yoe yuu jee mah?)

What is the temperature?
Wendu you duoshao?
(Wun-duu yoe dwaw-shou?)

Eating and Drinking

There is a saying in China that "food is heaven," and few, if any, people enjoy eating more than the Chinese. Because of the size of the country and such regional differences as climate and proximity to rivers, lakes, and the sea, there are corresponding differences in regional cuisines, with several major schools of cooking and dozens of smaller ones.

Chinese food	Zhong can	(Joong tsahn)
restaurant	fanguan	(fahn-gwahn)
big or name restaurant	fan zhuang	(fahn jwahng)
hotel restaurant	fan dian	(fahn dee-in)
coffee shop	kafei ting	(kah-fay teeng)
cafeteria-type restaurant	can guan	(tsahn gwahn)

dining car (train)	can che	(tsahn chuh)
snack bar	xiaochi dian	(shee-ow-chee dee-in)
Chinese snack bar	fengwei xiaochi	(fuung-way shee-ow-chee)
Beijing restaurant	Beifang guan	(Bay-fahng gwahn)
Cantonese restaurant	Guangdong guan	(Gwahng-doong gwahn)
Hunan restaurant	Hunan guan	(Huu-nahn gwahn)
Moslem restaurant	Qingzhen guan	(Cheeng-jun gwahn)
Shanghai restaurant	Shanghai guan	(Shahng-high gwahn)
Shangdong restaurant	Shandong guan	(Shahn-doong gwahn)
Szechuan restaurant	Sichuan guan	(Suh-chwahn gwahn)
cooking styles	pengtiao ban	(puung-tee-ow bahn)
barbecued	tanhuokao	(tahn-hwaw-kow)

braised	ganshao	(gahn-shou)
broil, roast	kao	(kow)
deep-fried	jiaozha	(jee-ow-jah)
fry	zha jian chao	(jah); (jee-in); (chow)
saute	chao	(chow)
stir-fried	bao-chao	(bow-chow)
steamed	qingzheng	(cheeng-juung)
Western food	Xi can	(She tsahn)
American food	Meiguo can	(May-gwaw tsahn)
eat	chi	(chee)
eat one's fill	chi bao	(chee bow)
drink	he	(huh)
breakfast	zaocan	(zow-tsahn)
lunch	wucan	(wuu-tsahn)
dinner	wancan	(wahn-tsahn)

snack	xiaochi	(shee-ow-chee)
reservations	yuding	(yuu-deeng)
make reservations	ding	(deeng)
counter	guitai	(gway-tie)
table	zhuozi	(jwaw-dzu)
VIP room	neiyou yazuo	(nay-yoe yah-zwaw)
younger waiter/ waitress	fuwuyuan	(fuu-wuu-ywen)
older waiter/ waitress	shifu	(shr-fuu)
menu	caidan	(tsigh-dahn)
English menu	Yingyu caidan	(Eeng-yuu tsigh-dahn)
appetizers	kaiweipin	(kigh-way-peen)
chopsticks	kuaizi	(kwie-dzu)
cup	beizi	(bay-dzu)
fork	chazi	(chah-dzu)

glass, drinking	boli beizi	(bwo-lee bay-dzu)
knife	daozi	(dow-dzu)
plate	pan	(pahn)
napkin	canjin	(tsahn-jeen)
spoon	shaozi	(shou-dzu)
garlic	suan	(swahn)
ginger	jiang	(jee-ahng)
salt	yan	(yahn)
pepper	hujiao	(huu-jee-ow)
pepper oil	lajiao you	(lah-jee-ow yoe)
chili pepper	lajiao fen	(lah-jee-ow fin)
sesame oil	xiang you	(shee-ahng yoe)
soy sauce	jiangyou	(jee-ahng-yoe)
sugar	tang	(tahng)
cold (to touch)	leng	(luung)
fresh	xinxian-de	(sheen-shee-in-duh)

frozen	dong-de	(doong-duh)
hot (to touch)	re	(ruh)
hot (spicy)	la-de	(lah-duh)
take home	daihui jia	(die-hway jee-ah)
rice, cooked	mifan	(me-fahn)
fried rice	fan chaofan	(fahn chow-fahn)

Meat   Rou (Roh)

beef	niurou	(neo-roe)
chicken	ji	(jee)
duck	yazi	(yah-dzu)
goose	e	(uh)
lamb	yangrou	(yahng-roe)
mutton	yangrou	(yahng-roe)
pheasant	yeji	(yeh-jee)
pigeon	gezi	(guh-dzu)
pork	zhurou	(juu-roe)
quail	anchun	(ahn-chwun)

| spare ribs | pai gu | (pie guu) |
| turkey | houji | (hoe-jee) |

Steak   Niupai (Neo-pie)

well-done	shou yi dian	(show ee dee-in)
medium	meijiewu	(may-jee-eh-wuu)
rare	bansheng banshu-de	(bahn-shuung); (bahn-shuu-duh)

Fish/Seafood   Yu (Yuu)/Haiwei (High-way)

abalone	baoyu	(bow-yuu)
bream	bianyu	(bee-in-yuu)
carp	liyu	(lee-yuu)
cod	xueyu	(shu-eh-yuu)
crab	pangxie	(pahng-she-eh)
cuttlefish	youyu	(yoe-yuu)
eel	manyu	(mahn-yuu)
lobster	longxia	(loong-shee-ah)

mackerel	qingyu	(cheeng-yuu)
mandarin fish	guiyu	(gway-yuu)
oysters	hao	(how)
perch	luyu	(luu-yuu)
prawns	daxia	(dah-shee-ah)
salmon	guiyu	(gway-yuu)
scallops	shanbeike	(shahn-bay-kuh)
shark's fin	yuchi	(yuu-chee)
shrimp	xia	(shee-ah)
sole	tayu	(tah-yuu)
squid	youyu	(yoe-yuu)
sturgeon	huangyu	(hwahng-yuu)
turbot	pingyu	(peeng-yuu)
yellow croaker	da huangyu	(dah hwahng-yuu)

Fruit   Shuiguo (Shway-gwaw)

apples	pin guo	(peen-gwaw)
apricots	xing	(sheeng)

159

bananas	xiangjiao	(shee-ahng-jee-ow)
dates	zaozi	(zow-dzu)
figs	wuhuaguo	(wuu-hwah-gwaw)
grapes	putao	(puu-tou)
lichee	lizhi	(lee-jr)
mango	mangguo	(mahng-gwaw)
muskmelon	hamigua	(hah-me-gwah)
oranges	juzi	(juu-dzu)
papaya	mugua	(muu-gwah)
peaches	taozi	(tou-dzu)
pears	lishu	(lee-shuu)
persimmons	shizi	(shr-dzu)
pineapples	fengli	(fuung-lee)
plums	lizi	(lee-dzu)
prunes	meizi	(may-dzu)
raisins	putaogan	(puu-tou-gahn)
raspberries	mumei	(muu-may)

strawberries	caomei	(tsow-may)
tangerines	juzi	(juu-dzu)
water chestnuts	biqi	(bee-chee)
watermelon	xigua	(she-gwaw)

Soup   Tang (Tahng)

beancurd and vege-table soup	qingcai doufu tang	(cheeng-tsigh doe-fuu tahng)
beef soup	niurou tang	(neo-roe tahng)
cabbage soup	baicai tang	(buy-tsigh tahng)
chicken soup	ji tang	(jee tahng)
crab soup	xierou tang	(she-eh-roe tahng)
fish soup	yu tang	(yuu tahng)
hot and sour soup	suan la tang	(swahn lah tahng)
shark's fin soup	yuchi tang	(yuu-chee tahng)
spicy vegetable soup	zhacai tang	(jah-tsigh tahng)

tomato and egg soup	xihongshi dan tang	(she-hoong-shr dahn tahng)
vegetable soup	zhacai tang	(jah-tsigh tahng)
winter melon soup	donggua tang	(doong-gwah tahng)

Vegetables Shucai (Shuu-tsigh)

asparagus	longxu	(loong-shu)
bamboo shoots	zhusun	(juu-suun)
bean curd	doufu	(doe-fuu)
beans	dou	(doe)
bean sprouts	douya	(doe-yah)
broccoli	gailan	(guy-lahn)
chili	lijiao	(lee-jee-ow)
cabbage	baicai	(buy-tsigh)
carrots	huluobo	(huu-lwaw-bwo)
celery	qincai	(cheen-tsigh)
coriander	xiancai	(shee-in-tsigh)
cucumber	huanggua	(hwahng-gwah)

eggplant	qiezi	(chee-eh-dzu)
garlic	suan	(swahn)
ginger	jiang	(jee-ahng)
green onions	cong	(tsoong)
green peppers	qing jiao	(cheeng jee-ow)
kidney beans	yao dou	(yow doe)
lettuce	shengcai	(shuung-tsigh)
mushrooms	mogu	(mwo-guu)
peanuts	huasheng	(hwah-shuung)
peas	wandou	(wahn-doe)
potatoes	tudou	(tuu-doe)
spinach	bocai	(bwo-tsigh)
spring onions	cong	(tsoong)
string beans	siji dou	(suh-jee doe)
tomatoes	xihongshi	(she-hoong-shr)
vegetarian	chisu sushizhe	(chee-suu); (suu-shr-juh)

I am a vegetarian.
Wo shi chisu-de.
(Waw shr chee-suu-duh.)

I don't eat meat.
Wo bu chi rou.
(Waw buu chee roe.)

American-style Breakfast
Meiguo Zaofan
(May-gwaw Zow-fahn)

coffee	kafei	(kah-fay)
cream	naiyou	(nigh-yoe)
tea	cha	(chah)
orange juice	juzi zhi	(juu-dzu jr)
eggs (chicken)	jidan	(jee-dahn)
boiled eggs	zhu jidan	(juu jee-dahn)
fried eggs	jian dan	(jee-in dahn)
poached eggs	zhu dan	(juu dahn)
scrambled eggs	chao jidan	(chow jee-dahn)
bread, rolls	mianbao	(mee-in-bow)

toast	kao mianbao	(kow mee-in-bow)
honey	fengmi	(fuung-me)
jam	guojiang	(gwaw-jee-ahng)

American-style Sandwiches
Meiguo Sanmingzhi
(May-gwaw Sahn-meeng-jr)

cheeseburger	nailao hanbaobao	(nigh-lou hahn-bow-bow)
cheese sandwich	nailao sanmingzhi	(nigh-lou sahn-meeng-jr)
hamburger	hanbaobao	(hahn-bow-bow)
ham sandwich	huotui sanmingzhi	(hwaw-tway sahn-meeng-jr)

American-style Desserts
Meiguo Tianshi
(May-gwaw Tee-in-shr)

cake	bing	(beeng)
ice cream	bing chilin	(beeng chee-leen)

fresh fruit	xinxian shuiguor	(sheen-shee-in shway-gwaw-urr)
pie	xianbing pie	(shee-in-beeng); (pee-eh)

Chinese Appetizers
Youming Zhongguo Kaiwei Xiaocai
(Yoe-meeng Joong-gwaw Kigh-way Shee-ow-tsigh)

braised bamboo shoots	youmen sun	(yoe-mun suun)
cold chicken	baiqieji	(buy-chee-eh-jee)
cold platter (mixed)	leng pan	(luung pahn)
fish jelly	ban haizhe	(bahn high-juh)
jellyfish	haizhe pi	(high-juh pee)
marinated beef	jiang niurou	(jee-ahng neo-roe)
preserved duck eggs	songhua dan	(soong-hwah dahn)
pickled mustard greens	la cai	(lah tsigh)
salted duck	yanshui ya	(yahn-shway yah)

| salted peanuts | xian huasheng | (shee-in hwah-shuung) |
| spicy pickled cabbage | la baicai | (lah buy-tsigh) |

Chinese Chicken and Duck Dishes
Youming Zhongguo Ji gen Yazi Cai
(Yoe-meeng Joong-gwaw Jee gun
Yah-dzu Tsigh)

Beijing (Peking) duck	Beijing kaoya	(bay-jeeng kow-yah)
begger's chicken	jiaohua ji	(jee-ow-hwah jee)
chicken stir-fried with peanuts and chilis	gongbao jiding	(goong-bow jee-deeng)
chicken in pepper and sesame sauce	guaiwei ji	(gwie-way jee)
crisp-fried duck	xiangsu ya	(shee-ahng-suu-yah)
crisp-fried chicken	xiangsu ji	(shee-ahng-suu jee)
marinated chicken breast, stir-fried	jiangbao jiding	(jee-ahng-bow jee-deeng)

167

Fish Dishes
Youming Yu Cai
(Yoe-meeng Yuu Tsigh)

braised fish with chilis and bean sauce	ganshao yu	(gahn-shou yuu)
"red" fish braised in soy sauce	hongshao yu	(hoong-shou yuu)
steamed fish marinated in soy sauce with garlic and spring onions	qingzheng yu	(cheeng-juung-yuu)
sweet and sour fish	tangcu yu	(tahng-tsu yuu)

Pork Dishes
Youming Rou Cai
(Yoe-meeng Roe Tsigh)

boiled pork spiced and stir-fried	huiguo rou	(hway-gwaw roe)
diced pork with chilis	lazi rouding	(lah-dzu roe-deeng)
pork meatballs and cabbage	shizi tou	(shr-dzu toe)
shredded pork, garlic, ginger, and chilis	yuxiang rousi	(yuu-shee-ahng roe-suh)

shredded pork and mushrooms	muer rou	(muu-urr roe)
sweet-and-sour pork	gulao rou	(guu-lou roe)
sweet-and-sour pork ribs	tancu paigu	(tahn-tsu pie-guu)

Vegetable Dishes
Youming Shu Cai
(Yoe-meeng Shuu Tsigh)

bean curd cooked red	hongshao doufu	(hoong-shou doe-fuu)
braised eggplant	shao qiezi	(shou chee-eh-dzu)
broccoli stir-fried	chao ganlan	(chow gahn-lahn)
mixed vegetables stir-fried	chao shijin shucai	(chow shr-jeen shuu-tsigh)
mushrooms and cauliflower stir-fried	xiami caihua	(shee-ah-me tsigh-hwah)
mushrooms and vegetables stir-fried	shao er dong	(shou urr doong)

169

Chinese Soups*
Youming Zhongguo Tang
(Yoe-meeng Joong-gwaw Tahng)

chicken soup	ji tang	(jee tahng)
egg-drop soup	jidan tang	(jee-dahn tahng)
egg and tomato soup	xihongshi jidan tang	(she-hoong-shr jee-dahn tahng)
hot-and-sour soup	suanla tang	(swahn-lah tahng)
pickled vegetable soup	zhacai tang	(jah-tsigh tahng)

Dim Sum Dishes
Youming Dim Sum Cai
(Yoe-meeng Dim Suum Tsigh)

Dim sum, a Cantonese specialty, consists of small, individual portions of dozens of popular Cantonese dishes, served on saucers or in small baskets. In the typical dim sum restaurant, servers push dim sum–laden carts around the restaurant (or carry trays) so diners can name or point to what they want. A full dim sum meal for an individual may consist of up to eight or more dishes.

---

* Usually eaten at the end of the meal.

steamed buns stuffed with sweetened bean paste	dou sha bao	(doe shah bow)
shrimp dumplings	xia jiao	(shee-ah jee-ow)
spring rolls	chun juan	(chwun jwen)
small steamed pork buns	xiao long bao	(shee-ow loong bow)
steamed pork dumplings	shao mai	(shou my)
steamed buns stuffed with roast pork	cha shao bao	(chah shou bow)
sweetened rice stuffed with meat in lotus leaves	nuo mi zongzi	(nwaw me zoong-dzu)
turnip cake	luo bo gao	(lwaw bwo gow)
wontons	hun tun	(hwun twun)

Chinese Desserts
Youming Zhongguo Tianshi
(Yoe-meeng Joong-gwaw Tee-in-shr)

| almond buns | xingren su | (sheeng-wren suu) |
| almond gelatin | xingren doufu | (sheeng-wren doe-fuu) |

bean-curd in ginger-flavored sweetened water	doufu hua	(doe-fuu hwah)
date-filled buns	zaoni bing	(zow-nee beeng)
"eight treasure rice"	babao fan	(bah-bow fahn)
hot-candied apples	basi pingguo	(bah-suh peeng-gwaw)
lotus-paste cakes	yue bing	(yu-eh beeng)
sesame cream	zhima hu	(jr-mah huu)
sesame crisp cake	zhima bing	(jr-mah beeng)
steamed bun stuffed with red-bean paste	dousha bao	(doe-shah bow)

Expressions

delicious	haochi-de	(how-chee-duh)
It tastes good.	Kekou.	(Kuh-koe.)
No more, thanks.	Gou-le, xiexie.	(Go-luh, she-eh-she-eh.)
It tastes bad.	Fu kekou.	(Fuu kuh-koe.)
toothpick	yaqian	(yah-chee-in)

I'm hungry.
Wo ele.
(Waw uh-luh.)

I would like to eat Western food.
Wo xiang chi Xican.
(Waw shee-ahng chee She-tsahn.)

There are three of us.
Wo-men san ge ren.
(Waw-mun sahn guh wren.)

Can you make an American-style breakfast?
Ni keyi zuo Meiguo shi zao can ma?
(Nee kuh-ee zwaw May-gwaw shr zow tsahn mah?)

Do you have an English-language menu?
You Yingwen caidan ma?
(Yoe Eeng-wun tsigh-dahn mah?)

Tea with milk, please.
Qing zai cha zhong jia dian nai.
(Cheeng zigh chah joong jee-ah dee-in nigh.)

What kind of fish is this?
Zhe shi shenme yu?
(Juh shr shuun-muh yuu?)

What is that?
Na shi shenme?
(Nah shr shuun-muh?)

Please give me _____.
Qing gei wo _____.
(Cheeng gay waw _____.)

Please bring me _____.
Qing na gei wo _____.
(Cheeng nah gay waw _____.)

Please bring me another one (one more).
Qing zai lai yige.
(Cheeng zigh lie ee-guh.)

What kind of dessert do you have?
Ni xiang yao shenme dianxin?
(Nee shee-ahng yow shuun-muh dee-in-sheen?)

Thank you for the delicious meal.
Xiexie fan tai xiong.
(She-eh-she-eh fahn tie shee-ong.)

Drinks

drink (noun)	yinliao	(een-lee-ow)
to drink (verb)	he	(huh)
bar	jiuba	(jeo-bah)
café	leng yindian	(luung een-dee-in)
coffee shop	kafei ting	(kah-fay teeng)
teahouse	chaguan	(chah-gwahn)

Chinese alcoholic drinks

maotai	(mou-tie), a powerful brew made from sorghum

174

shaoxing jiu   (shou-sheeng jeo), a rice wine

wu-liang ye   (wuu-lee-ahng yeh), a five-grain liquor

Western alcoholic drinks

beer	pijiu	(pee-jeo)
black beer	hei pijiu	(hay pee-jeo)
brandy	bailandi	(buy-lahn-dee)
champagne	xiangbin	(shee-ahng-bin)
draft beer	zha pi	(jah pee)
cocktail	jiweijin	(jee-way-jeen)
gin	dusongzijin	(duu-soong-dzu-jeen)
highball	weishijijiu	(way-shr-jee-jeo)
martini	matini	(mah-tee-nee)
scotch	sigete	(suh-guh-tuh)
vodka	futejia	(fuu-tuh-jee-ah)
whisky	weishiji	(way-shr-jee)
on the rocks	jia bingkuai	(jee-ah beeng-kwie)

175

straight	bu jia bingkuai	(buu jee-ah beeng-kwie)
whisky with water	weishiji jia shui	(way-shr-jee jee-ah shway)
wine	putaojiu	(puu-tou-jeo)
hangover	zui	(zway)
Cheers!	Ganbei!	(Gahn-bay!)

Soft drinks   Qishui (Chee-shway)

cold drink	leng yin	(luung een)
apple juice	ping guozhi	(peeng gwaw-jr)
boiled water	kai shui	(kigh shwee)
black tea	hong cha	(hoong chah)
brown tea	wulong cha	(wuu-loong chah)
green tea	lu cha	(luu chah)
jasmine tea	molihua cha	(mwo-lee-hwah chah)
Coca Cola	Kekoukele	(Kuh-koe-kuh-luh)
coffee (black)	kafei	(kah-fay)

coffee, with cream	kafei, jia niunai	(kah-fay, jee-ah neo-nigh)
hot chocolate	re qiaokeli	(ruh chee-ow-kuh-lee)
lemonade	qishui	(chee-shway)
milk	niunai	(neo-nigh)
cold milk	leng niunai	(luung neo-nigh)
mineral water	kuangquan shui	(kwahng-chwahn-shway)
fresh orange juice	xian juzhi	(shee-in juu-jr)
Pepsi Cola	Pepsi Kele	(Pepsi Kuh-luh)
tea with lemon	ningmeng cha	(neeng-muung chah)
tea with milk	hongcha jia niunai	(hoong-chah jee-ah neo-nigh)
tomato juice	xihongshi zhi	(she-hoong-shr jr)
water	shui	(shway)

I'm thirsty.
Wo kele.
(Waw kuh-luh.)

Chinese beer, please.
Qing na Zhongguo pijiu.
(Cheeng nah Joong-gwaw pee-jeo.)

Do you have draft beer?
Ni you zha bijiu?
(Nee yoe jah bee-jeo?)

Another round, please.
Qing zai lai yi-ge.
(Cheeng zigh lie ee-guh.)

Some tidbits (peanuts, and so on), please.
Qing cheng yi dian.
(Cheeng chuung ee dee-in.)

Would you like tea?
Ni xihuan he cha ma?
(Nee she-hwahn huh chah mah?)

Please bring me _____.
Qing gei wo _____.
(Cheeng gay waw _____.)

Paying bills

bill, check	zhangdan	(jahng-dahn)
separate checks	fenkai suan	(fin-kigh swahn)
receipt	shouju	(show-juu)
mistake	cuowu	(tswaw-wuu)
credit card	shinyong ka	(sheen-yoong kah)

The bill, please.
Qing suan zhang.
(Cheeng swahn jahng.)

A receipt, please.
Qing suan shouju.
(Cheeng swahn show-juu.)

Is a credit card okay?
Shingyong ka keyi ma?
(Sheeng-yoong kah kuh-ee mah?)

Telephone and Fax
Telephone

telephone	dianhua	(dee-in-hwah)
make a call	da dianhua	(dah dee-in-hwah)
local call	bendi dianhua	(bin-dee dee-in-hwah)
domestic call	guonei dianhua	(gwaw-nay dee-in-hwah)
long-distance call	changtu dianhua	(chahng-tuu dee-in-hwah)
international call	guowai dianhua	(gwaw-wigh dee-in-hwah)
public telephone	gongyong dianhua	(goong-yoong dee-in-hwah)

179

in-house phone	nei xian dianhua	(nay shee-in dee-in-hwah)
collect call	shouhuaren fufei dianhua	(show-hwah-wren fuu-fay dee-in-hwah)
operator	zhongji	(joong-jee)
person-to-person	jiaoren dianhua	(jee-ow-wren dee-in-hwah)
telephone number	dianhua haoma	(dee-in-hwah how-mah)
telephone directory	dianhua bu	(dee-in-hwah buu)
extension	fenxian fenji	(fin-shee-in); (fin-jee)
busy signal	zhanxianle	(jahn-shee-in-luh)
hello	wei	(way)
message	liuhua	(leo-hwah)
goodbye	zaijian	(zigh-jee-in)

I would like to speak with _____.
Wo zhao _____.
(Waw jow _____.)

Communicating in Chinese

I want to make an international call.
Wo yao da yige guoji changtu dianhua.
(Waw yow dah ee-guh gwaw-jee chahng-tuu dee-in-hwah.)

I want to make a collect call.
Wo xiang qing duifang fuqian.
(Waw shee-ahng cheeng dway-fahng fuu-chee-in.)

What is your telephone number?
Ni-de dianhua haoma shi?
(Nee-duh dee-in-hwah how-mah shr?)

My telephone number is _____.
Wo-de dianhua haoma shi _____.
(Waw duh dee-in-hwah how-mah shr _____.)

You have a phone call.
Ni yan yi-ge dianhua.
(Nee yahn ee-guh dee-in-hwah.)

Just a moment, please.
Qing deng yi xia.
(Cheeng duung ee shee-ah.)

Who is calling, please?
Qing wen nin shi shei?
(Cheeng wun neen shr shay?)

Is Mr. Zhang in?
Zhang Xiansheng zaime?
(Jahng Shee-in-shuung zigh-muh?)

He is away from his desk.
Ta likai ta-de ban gongzhuo.
(Tah lee-kigh tah-duh bahn goong-jwaw.)

He/she is out now.
Ta xian zai chu qu-le.
(Tah shee-in zigh chuu chu-luh.)

He/she is on another line.
Ta xian zai zheng zai da dianhua.
(Tah shee-in zigh juung zigh dah dee-in-hwah.)

He/she is in a meeting.
Ta xian zai zai kaihui.
(Tah shee-in zigh zigh kigh-hway.)

Shall I have him/her call you?
Wo nang ta da dianhua gei ni hao ma?
(Waw nahng tah dah dee-in-hwah gay nee how mah?)

Please tell him I called.
Qing gaosu ta wo-de dianhua.
(Cheeng gow-suu tah waw-duh dee-in-hwah.)

May I use your phone?
Keyi yong ni-de dianhua ma?
(Kuh-ee yoong nee-duh dee-in-hwah mah?)

Fax

fax	chuanzhenji	(chwahn-jun-jee)
fax number	chuanzhenji haoma	(chwahn-jun-jee how-mah)
fax paper	chuanzhenji zhi	(chwahn-jun-jee jr)
send a fax	fa chuanzhen	(fah chwahn-jun)

182

I want to send a fax.
Xiang da tuwen chuanzhen.
(Shee-ahng dah tuu-wun chwahn-jun.)

I will fax you tomorrow.
Wo mingtian chuanzhen gei ni.
(Waw meeng-tee-in chwahn-jun gay nee.)

Are there any faxes for me?
Zhe li you wo-de chuanzhen ma?
(Juh lee yoe waw-duh chwahn-jun mah?)

Shopping

shop, store	shangdian	(shahng-dee-in)
shopping	mai dongxi	(my doong-she)
shopping center	shang chang shangpin bu	(shahng chahng); (shahng-peen buu)
shopping street	gouwu jie	(go-wuu jee-eh)
department store	baihuo shangdian	(buy-hwaw shahng-dee-in)
Friendship Store	Youyi Shangdian	(Yoe-ee Shahng-dee-in)
souvenir shop	luyou jinianpin shangdian	(luu-yoe jee-nee-in-peen shahng-dee-in)

bookstore	shu dian	(shuu dee-in)
free market	ziyou shichang	(dzu-yoe shr-chahng)
business hours	yingye shijian	(eeng-yeh shr-jee-in)
buy	mai	(my)

(I) want to buy _____.
Xiang mai _____.
(Shee-ahng my _____.)

(I) want to see _____.
Xiang kankan _____.
(Shee-ahng kahn-kahn _____.)

Please show me _____.
Qing gei wo kankan _____.
(Cheeng gay waw kahn-kahn _____.)

have	you	(yoe)

Do you have _____?
Ni you _____?
(Nee yoe _____?)

How much (is it)?
Duoshao qian?
(Dwaw-shou chee-in?)

too expensive	tai gui-le	(tie gway-luh)
cheap	pianyi	(pee-in-ee)

cheaper	gengpianyi	(guung-pee-in-ee)
cheapest	zuipianyi	(zway-pee-in-ee)
large, big	da	(dah)
larger	geng da jiao da-de	(guung dah); (jee-ow dah-duh)
largest	zuida	(zway-dah)
small, little	xiao	(shee-ow)
smaller	geng xiao jiao xiao-de	(guung shee-ow); (jee-ow shee-ow- duh)
smallest	zuixiao	(zway-shcc-ow)
gift	liwu	(lee-wuu)

I want to buy a gift.
Wo xiang mai liwu.
(Waw shee-ahng my lee-wuu.)

jewelry	shoushi	(show-shr)
leather	pi ge	(pee); (guh)
discount	zhekou	(juh-koe)

Will you give (me) a discount?
Neng da zhekou ma?
(Nuung dah juh-koe mah?)

exchange (verb)	huan	(hwahn)

Can you exchange this?
Neng huan yige ma?
(Nuung hwahn ee-guh mah?)

written instructions	shuoming shu	(shwaw-meeng shuu)
summer gift-giving season	xia ji songli jijie	(shee-ah jee soong-lee jee-jee-eh)
year-end gift-giving season	nian zhong songli jijie	(nee-in joong soong-lee jee-jee-eh)
call to a female clerk (Miss!)	Xiaojie!	(Shee-ow-jee-eh!)
call to any clerk	Shifu!	(Shr-fuu!)
calligraphy	shufa	(shuu-fah)
carpets	ditan	(dee-tahn)
cloisonne	jingtailan	(jeeng-tie-lahn)
fabrics	buliao	(buu-lee-ow)
jewelry	shoushi	(show-shr)
lacquerware	qiqi	(chee-chee)

paintings	hua	(hwah)
porcelain	ciqi	(tsu-chee)
pottery	taoqi	(tou-chee)
silk goods	sizhi pin	(suh-jr peen)
stone rubbings	mo tuoben	(mwo twaw-bin)

I would like to buy _____.
Xiang mai _____.
(Shee-ahng my _____.)

Where can I buy _____?
Zai nar neng mai _____?
(Zigh nah-urr nuung my _____?)

Let's go shopping tomorrow.
Women mingtian qu mai huo.
(Waw-mun meeng-tee-in chu my hwaw.)

I want to go shopping this afternoon.
Wo xiawu qu mai huo.
(Waw shee-ah-wuu chu my hwaw.)

Let me see that, please.
Qing rang wo kanyikan na-ge.
(Cheeng rahng waw kahn-ee-kahn nah-guh.)

May I try it on?
Wo keyi shiyishi ma?
(Waw kuh-ee shr-ee-shr mah?)

Are there other colors?
You bie-de yanse ma?
(Yoe bee-eh-duh yahn-suh mah?)

I would like to buy a gift.
Wo xiang mai yi jian liwu.
(Waw shee-ahng my ee jee-in lee-wuu.)

I am looking for a leather purse.
Wo zheng zai zhao yi-ge pi qian bao.
(Waw juung zigh jow ee-guh pee chee-in bow.)

Will you give me a discount?
Ni neng gei wo jiang dian jia?
(Nee nuung gay waw jee-ahng dee-in jee-ah?)

It doesn't fit.
Bu heshi.
(Buu huh-shr.)

It's too big.
Tai da-le.
(Tie dah-luh.)

It's too small.
Tai xiao-le.
(Tie shee-ow-luh.)

Do you have a smaller one?
Ni you xiao yi dian-de ma?
(Nee yoe shee-ow ee dee-in-duh mah?)

This one is too expensive.
Zhe ge shi tai gui.
(Juh guh shr tie gway.)

Have you a cheaper one?
Ni you pianyi-de ma?
(Nee yoe pee-in-ee-duh mah?)

I'm just looking.
Xian kankan.
(Shee-in kahn-kahn.)

Business Matters

business	shengyi	(shuung-ee)
businessperson	shangren	(shahng-wren)
office	bangongshi	(bahn-goong-shr)
office hours	bangongshi jian	(bahn-goong-shr jee-in)
office building	bangong-de lou	(bahn-goong-duh low)
high-rise building	muotian-de she	(mwaw-tee-in-duh shuh)
address	dizhi	(dee-jr)
appointment	yuehui	(yu-eh-hway)
conference, meeting	huiyi	(hway-ee)
conference room	huiyi shi	(hway-ee shr)

floor	ceng	(tsuung)
company	gongsi	(goong-suh)
workplace	danwei	(dahn-way)
president	zongcai	(zoong-tsigh)
factory manager	chang zhang	(chahng jahng)
general manager	zong jingli	(zoong jeeng-lee)
manager	jingli	(jeeng-lee)
engineer-in-chief	zong gongchengshi	(zoong goong-chuung-shr)
engineer	gongchengshi	(goong-chuung-shr)
workshop foreman	chejian zhuren	(chuh-jee-in juu-wren)
department manager	bu jingli	(buu jeeng-lee)
section manager	ke jingli	(kuh jeeng-lee)
supervisor	guanli ren	(gwahn-lee wren)
worker	gongren	(goong-wren)

factory	gongchang	(goong-chahng)
state-run factory	guo-ying gongchang	(gwaw-eeng goong-chahng)
trade union	gong hui	(goong hway)
foreign investment	waiguo touzi	(wigh-gwaw toe-dzu)
Sino-foreign JV	Zhong-wai hezi	(Joong-wigh huh-dzu)
bonus	jiangjin	(jee-ahng-jeen)
pension	tuixiujin	(tway-sheo-jeen)
wages	gongzi	(goong-dzu)

What is the name of your company?
Ni gongsi-de mingzi shi?
(Nee goong-suh-duh meeng-dzu shr?)

Where is your office?
Nili shi ni-de bangong shi?
(Nee-lee shr nee-duh bahn-goong shr?)

What is your address?
Ni-de zhu zhi shi?
(Nee-duh juu jr shr?)

Please write it down.
Qing xie xia lai.
(Cheeng she-eh shee-ah lie.)

What is your telephone number?
Ni-de dianhua haoma shi?
(Nee-duh dee-in-hwah how-mah shr?)

My telephone number is _____.
Wo-de dianhua haoma shi _____.
(Waw-duh dee-in-hwah how-mah shr _____.)

What floor is your office on?
Ni-de bangong shi zai ji ceng?
(Nee-duh bahn-goong shr zigh jee tsuung?)

I have an appointment with Mr. Zhang at ten o'clock.
Shidian, wo he Zhang Xiansheng you yi-ge yuehui.
(Shr-dee-in, waw huh Jahng Shee-in-shuung yoe ee-guh
    yu-eh-hway.)

Where will Mr. Wu's meeting be held?
Wu Xiansheng-de hui zai nali juxing?
(Wuu Shee-in-shuung-duh hway zigh nah-lee
    juu-sheeng?)

I would like to make an appointment with Mr. Lin.
Wo xiang he Lin Xiangsheng ding yi-ge yuehui.
(Waw shee-ahng huh Leen Shee-ahng-shuung deeng
    ee-guh yu-eh-hway.)

When will it be convenient for Mr. Lin?
Shenme shihou he Lin Xiangsheng tan hua?
(Shuun-muh shr-hoe huh Leen Shee-in-shuung tahn
    hwah?)

Will 2 P.M. tomorrow be all right?
Mingtian xia wu liangdian hao ma?
(Meeng-tee-in shee-ah wuu lee-ahng-dee-in how mah?)

I am waiting for Mr. Wang.
Wo zai deng Wang Xiansheng.
(Waw zigh duung Wahng Shee-in-shuung.)

May I use your phone?
Wo keyi yong ni-de dianhua ma?
(Waw kuh-ee yoong nee-duh dee-in-hwah mah?)

agreement	xieyi	(she-eh-ee)
capital	zijin	(dzu-jeen)
catalog	mulu	(muu-luu)
commission	yongjin	(yoong-jeen)
customer	kehu	(kuh-huu)
economy	jingji	(jeeng-jee)
equipment	shebei	(shuh-bay)
exhibit	zhanlanpin	(jahn-lahn-peen)
export	chukou	(chuu-koe)
firm offer	shi pan	(shr pahn)
final offer	zuizhong pan	(zway-joong pahn)
foreign trade	wai mao	(wigh mou)
freight	yunfei	(ywun-fay)

import	jinkou	(jeen-koe)
insurance	baoxianfei	(bow-shee-in-fay)
joint venture	hezi jingying	(huh-dzu jeeng-eeng)
letter of credit	xin yong zhang	(sheen yoong jahng)
loan	daikuan	(die-kwahn)
negotiate	tanpan	(tahn-pahn)
place an order	dinghuo	(deeng-hwaw)
plan	jihua	(jee-hwah)
policy	zheng ce	(juung tsuh)
price list	jiage dan	(jee-ah-guh dahn)
quotation	baojia	(bow-jee-ah)
trade show	jiaoyi hui	(jee-ow-ee hway)

At the Post Office

mail, postal matter	youjian	(yoe-jee-in)
post office	you ju	(yoe juu)
postage stamp	you piao	(yoe pee-ow)

postcard	mingxinpian	(meeng-sheen-pee-in)
envelope	xinfeng	(sheen-fuung)
letter	xinjian	(sheen-jee-in)
aerogram	hangkongxinjian	(hahng-koong-sheen-jee-in)
airmail	hangyou	(hahng-yoe)
airmail stamp	hangkong youpiao	(hahng-koong yoe-pee-ow)
surface mail	pingyou	(peeng-yoe)
express mail	kuaidi youjian	(kwie-dee yoe-jee-in)
registered letter	guahao xin	(gwah-how sheen)
special delivery	xianshi zhuansong	(shee-in-shr jwahn-soong)
parcel, package	baoguo	(bow-gwaw)
mail (send)	ji xin	(jee sheen)
weight	zhongliang	(joong-lee-ahng)
overweight	chao zhong	(chow joong)

glue	jiaoshui	(jee-ow-shway)
sealed	fengkou	(fuung-koe)
mail or post box	you tong you xiang	(yoe toong); (yoe shee-ahng)
address	dizhi	(dee-jr)
addressee	shouxinren	(show-sheen- wren)
mailman	youdiyuan	(yoe-dee-ywen)
zip code	youzheng bianma	(yoe-juung bee-in-mah)

Where is the nearest post office?
Zuijin-de you ju zai nali?
(Zway-jeen-duh yoe juu zigh nah-lee?)

What time does the post office open?
You ju jidian kaimen?
(Yoe juu jee-dee-in kigh-mun?)

What time does it close?
Nali jidian guanmen?
(Nah-lee jee-dee-in gwahn-mun?)

Please mail this.
Qing ji zhe jian.
(Cheeng jee juh jee-in.)

How much will it cost to send this by seamail?
Haiyun duoshao qian?
(High-ywun dwaw-shou chee-in?)

Ten aerogram forms, please.
Shi-ge hangkong xinfeng.
(Shr-guh hahng-koong sheen-fuung.)

How many days will it take to London?
Dao London duo cheng shi jian?
(Dow Loon-doon dwaw chuung shr jee-in?)

Health Matters

Western medicine	Xi yao	(She yow)
Western-style hospital	Xixi yuan	(She-she ywen)
Chinese medicine	Zhong yao	(Joong yow)
Chinese-style hospital	Zhongyi yuan	(Joong-ee ywen)
sick	shengbingle	(shuung-beeng-luh)
doctor	daifu yisheng	(die-fuu); (ee-shuung)
ambulance	jiuhuche	(jeo-huu-chuh)
hospital	yiyuan	(ee-ywen)

emergency room	jizhen shi	(jee-jun shr)
outpatient department	menzhen bu	(mun-jun buu)
clinic	zhensuo yiwushi	(jun-swaw); (ee-wuu-shr)
nurse	hushi	(huu-shr)
drugstore	yaodian	(yow-dee-in)
examination	jiancha	(jee-in-chah)
painful, hurts	teng	(tuung)
temperature	tiwen	(tee-wun)
bandage (noun)	bengdai	(buung-die)
bandage (verb)	baoza	(bow-zah)
operation	shoushu	(show-shuu)
infection	ganran	(gahn-rahn)
injection	dazhen	(dah-jun)
prescription	yaofang	(yow-fahng)
pill	yaowan	(yow-wahn)
allergy pills	guomin yao	(gwaw-meen yow)

eyedrops	yanyao	(yahn-yow)
x-ray	tou-shi	(toe-shr)
acupuncture	zhenjiu	(jun-jeo)
health insurance	jiankang baoxian	(jee-in-kahng bow-shee-in)
appendicitis	lanweiyan	(lahn-way-yahn)
asthma	xiaochuan	(shee-ow-chwahn)
bleeding	liu xue	(leo shu-eh)
chest cramp	xiongkou choujin	(shee-ong-koe choe-jeen)
a cold	shangfengle	(shahng-fuung-luh)
catch cold	ganmao-le	(gahn-mou-luh)
constipation	bianmi	(bee-in-me)
cough	kesou	(kuh-soe)
diarrhea	xieduzi	(shee-eh-duu-dzu)
dizzy	touyun	(toe-ywun)
dysentery	youliji	(yoe-lee-jee)

fever	fashao-le	(fah-shou-luh)
food poisoning	shiwu zhongdu-le	(shr-wuu joong-duu-luh)
flu	ganmao-le	(gahn-mou-luh)
headache	touteng	(toe-tuung)
hepatitis	ganyan	(gahn-yahn)
high blood pressure	xueya guo gao	(shu-eh-yah gwaw gow)
injury	shang	(shahng)
pneumonia	feiyan	(fay-yahn)
sore throat	houlong teng	(hoe-loong tuung)
stomachache	duzi teng	(duu-dzu tuung)
vomit	yizhitu	(ee-jr-tuu)
toothache	ya teng	(yah tuung)
dentist	yayi yake yisheng	(yah-ee); (yah-kuh ee-shuung)

I'm sick, please call a doctor.
Wo sheng bing-le, qing jiao yi-ge yisheng.
(Waw shuung beeng-luh, cheeng jee-ow ee-guh ee-shuung.)

Please call an ambulance.
Qing jiao jiuhuche.
(Cheeng jee-ow jeo-huu-chuh.)

(Someone) has been hurt in an accident.
_____ shou shang-le.
(_____ show shahng-luh.)

Please help me (us)!
Qing bang zhu wo (women)!
(Cheeng bahng juu waw [waw-mun]!)

I caught a cold.
Wo gan mao.
(Waw gahn mou.)

My head is aching, do you have any aspirin?
Wo tan teng, ni you asplin ma?
(Waw tahn tuung, nee yoe ahs-pleen mah?)

Please call a doctor who speaks English.
Qing yi wei jiang Yingyu-de yisheng.
(Cheeng ee way jee-ahng Eeng-yuu-duh ee-shuung.)

Housing Matters

apartment	yitao zhufang	(ee-tou juu-fahng)
house	fangzi	(fahng-dzu)
courtyard house	si he yuan	(suh huh ywen)
rent a place	zu fangzi	(zuu fahng-dzu)
the rent	fangzu	(fahng-zuu)

rental agent	dichan jingji ren	(dee-chahn jeeng-jee wren)
garden	huayuan	(hwah-ywen)
deposit	baozhengjin	(bow-juung-jeen)
guarantor	baozhengren	(bow-juung-wren)
kitchen	chufang	(chuu-fahng)
dining room	can shi	(tsahn shr)
bathroom	yushi	(yuu-shr)
view	fengjing	(fuung-jeeng)

I want to rent an apartment.
Wo xiang zu yi tao fangzi.
(Waw shee-ahng zuu ee tou fahng-dzu.)

How much is the monthly rent?
Duoshao qian yi-ge yue?
(Dwaw-shou chee-in ee-guh yu-eh?)

Does it have a view?
Neng kan dao feng jing?
(Nuung kahn dow fuung jeeng?)

Visiting a Home

invite	yaoqing	(yow-cheeng)
invitation	qingjian	(cheeng-jee-in)

home	jia	(jee-ah)
house	fangzi	(fahng-dzu)
address	dizhi	(dee-jr)
floor	ceng	(tsuung)
street	jie	(jee-eh)
road	lu	(luu)
map	ditu	(dee-tuu)
directions	fangxiang	(fahng-shee-ahng)
time	shijian	(shr-jee-in)

I would like to invite you to my home.
Wo xiang qing yi qu wo jia.
(Waw shee-ahng cheeng ee chu waw jee-ah.)

What time shall I come?
Ji dian wo keyi lai?
(Jee dee-in waw kuh-ee lie?)

Please come at 7 P.M.
Qing wansheng qidian lai.
(Cheeng wahn-shuung chee-dee-in lie.)

Thank you for the invitation.
Xiexie ni-de yao qing.
(She-eh-she-eh nee-duh yow cheeng.)

Thank you, I've had enough.
Xiexie, wo yi jin chi bao-le.
(She-eh-she-eh, waw ee jeen chee bow-luh.)

The meal was delicious.
Fan hen xiang.
(Fahn hin shee-ahng.)

Thank you for a wonderful evening.
Xiexie jintian wan hen gaoxin.
(She-eh-she-eh jeen-tee-in wahn hin gow-sheen.)

Don't mention it.
Bu keqi.
(Buu kuh-chee.)

You're welcome.
Huan yi ni.
(Hwahn ee nee.)

Entertainment and Recreation

acrobatic performance	kan zaji biaoyan	(kahn zah-jee bee-ow-yahn)
ballet	baleiwu	(bah-lay-wuu)
classical music concert	ting guoyue yanzou	(teeng gwaw-yu-eh yahn-zoe)
comic dialogue show	ting xiangsheng	(teeng shee-ahng-shuung)

concert	ting yinyue hui	(teeng een-yu-eh hway)
concert hall	yinyue ting	(een-yu-eh teeng)
local folk opera	kan difang xi	(kahn dee-fahng she)
magic show	kan moshu biaoyan	(kahn mwo-shuu bee-ow-yahn)
martial arts performance	kan wushu biaoyan	(kahn wuu-shuu bee-ow-yahn)
movie	dianying	(dee-in-eeng)
Chinese movie	Zhongguo pian	(Joong-gwaw pee-in)
Chinese historical drama	Zhongguo lishi pian	(Joong-gwaw lee-shr pee-in)
foreign movie	waiguo pian	(wigh-gwaw pee-in)
American movie	Meiguo pian	(May-gwaw pee-in)
kung fu film	wushu pian	(wuu-shuu pee-in)
documentary film	jilu pian	(jee-luu pee-in)

205

feature film	gushi pian	(guu-shr pee-in)
English subtitles	Yingwen zimu	(eeng-wun dzu-muu)
film festival	dian yingjie	(dee-in eeng-jee-eh)
puppet theater	mu ouxi	(muu oh-she)
theater	juchang	(juu-chahng)
a play	huaju	(hwah-juu)
opera	geju	(guh-juu)
Peking opera	Jing ju	(Jeeng juu)
program	jiemudan	(jee-eh-muu-dahn)
intermission	xiuxi	(sheo-she)
dance	wuhui	(wuu-hway)
disco	diske	(dees-kuh)

Sports Tiyu (Tee-yuu)

| baseball | bangqiu | (bahng-cheo) |
| basketball | lanqiu | (lahn-cheo) |

martial arts	wu shu	(wuu shuu)
ping-pong	pingpong qiu	(peeng-pong cheo)
soccer	zuqiu	(zuu-cheo)
softball	leiqiu	(lay-cheo)
swimming	youyong	(yoe-yoong)
tennis	wangqiu	(wahng-cheo)
volleyball	paiqiu	(pie-cheo)
game	youxi	(yoe-she)
score	bifen	(bee-fin)
court	bisai changdi	(bee-sigh chahng-dee)
team	dui	(dway)
lose	shu	(shuu)
win	ying	(eeng)
referee	caipanyuan	(tsigh-pahn-ywen)
friendship match	youyi sai	(yoe-ee sigh)
tournament	yaoqingsai	(yow-cheeng-sigh)

| playground | caochang | (tsow-chahng) |
| gymnasium | tiyuguan | (tee-yuu-gwahn) |

Beach   Haitan (High-tahn)

jellyfish	shuimu	(shway-muu)
sharks	shayu	(shah-yuu)
no swimming	jinzhi youyong	(jeen-jr yoe-yoong)

Swimming pool   Chi (Chee)

| lifeguard | jiushengyuan | (jeo-shuung-ywen) |
| shower | linyu | (leen-yuu) |

Sightseeing   Youlan (Yoe-lahn)

city map	shiqu ditu	(shr-chu dee-tuu)
local map	dangdi ditu	(dahng-dee dee-tuu)
art gallery	meishu guan	(may-shuu gwahn)
Buddhist temple	si miao	(suh); (mee-ow)
monument	jinianbei	(jee-nee-in-bay)
museum	bowuguan	(bwo-wuu-gwahn)

palace	gongdian	(goong-dee-in)
Taoist temple	guan	(gwahn)
far (distant)	yuan	(ywen)
close (nearby)	kuaiyao	(kwie-yow)
stroll, walk	sanbu	(sahn-buu)
square	guangchang	(gwahng-chahng)
street	jiedao	(jee-eh-dow)
main street	da jie	(dah jee-eh)
side street	hu tong	(huu toong)
pedestrian crossing	renxing hengdao	(wren-sheeng huung-dow)
traffic light	honglu deng	(hoong-luu duung)
bridge	qiao	(chee-ow)
river	he	(huh)
hill	xiaoshan	(shee-ow-shahn)
mountain	shan	(shahn)
Grand Canal	Da Yunhe	(Dah Ywun-huh)

I want to go somewhere this evening.
Jintian wansheng wo xiang qu yixie difang.
(Jeen-tee-in wahn-shuung waw shee-ahng chu
    ee-she-eh dee-fahng.)

Would you like to go with me?
Ni yuanyi he wo yiqi qu ma?
(Nee ywen-ee huh waw ee-chee chu mah?)

Where would you like to go?
Ni xiang qu rili?
(Nee shee-ahng chu rr-lee?)

Let's go to the opera.
Women qu yinyue ting.
(Waw-mun chu een-yu-eh teeng.)

I want to see a martial arts exhibition.
Wo xiang kan wushu biaoyan.
(Waw shee-ahng kahn wuu-shuu bee-ow-yahn.)

I'd like to do some sightseeing.
Wo xihuan youlan.
(Waw she-hwahn yoe-lahn.)

May I take photographs?
Wo nengbuneng zhaoxiang?
(Waw nuung-buu-nuung jah-oh-shee-ahng?)

May I take your photograph?
Wo keyi gei ni zhaoxiang ma?
(Waw kuh-ee gay nee jah-oh-shee-ahng mah?)

Shall we go by subway?
Women zuo ditie ma?
(Waw-mun zwaw dee-tee-eh mah?)

Let's go by taxi.
Women zuo chuzuche.
(Waw-mun zwaw chuu-zuu-chuh.)

Is it far from here?
Li zhe li yuan ma?
(Lee juh lee ywen mah?)

Is it near here?
Zai fujin ma?
(Zigh fuu-jeen mah?)

Is it near a subway station?
Zhe li you ditie zhan ma?
(Juh lee yoe dee-tee-eh jahn mah?)

Let's walk.
Women zou zhe qu.
(Waw-mun zoe juh chu.)

Let's take a stroll.
Women sanbu zhe qu.
(Waw-mun sahn-buu juh chu.)

I'm tired.
Wo leile.
(Waw lay-luh.)

I'm lost.
Wo milu le.
(Waw me-luu luh.)

Emergency Situations

passport	huzhao	(huu-jow)
money	qian	(chee-in)
bag	bao	(bow)
camera	zhaoxiangji	(jow-shee-ahng-jee)

I've had an accident!
There's been an accident!
Chushi-le!
(Chuu-shr-luh!)

I'm sick.
Wo shengbing-le.
(Waw shuung-beeng-luh.)

My husband/wife is sick.
Wo zhangfu/qizi shengbing-le.
(Waw jahng-fuu/chee-dzu shuung-beeng-luh.)

My friend is sick.
Wo pengyou shengbing-le.
(Waw puung-yoe shuung-beeng-luh.)

Please call a doctor!
Qing jiao yiwei yisheng!
(Cheeng jee-ow ee-way ee-shuung!)

I need to go to a hospital.
Wo xuyao qu yige yiyuan.
(Waw shu-yow chu ee-guh ee-ywen.)

Please call a doctor who speaks English.
Qing jiao yiwei jiang Yingwen-de yisheng.
(Cheeng jee-ow ee-way jee-ahng Eeng-wun-duh
     ee-shuung.)

Thief!   Xiaotou!   (Shee-ow-toe!)

I've been robbed.
Wo bei dajie-le.
(Waw bay dah-jee-eh-luh.)

I want to call my embassy.
Wo xiang gen wo-de dashiguan lianluo.
(Waw shee-ahng gun waw-duh dah-shr-gwahn
     lee-in-lwaw.)

Please call the police.
Qing jiao yingche.
(Cheeng jee-ow eeng-chuh.)

Toilets

As in English, there are several Chinese words used in
reference to toilet facilities.

toilet	cesuo	(tsuh-swaw)
washroom	xishou jian	(she-show jee-in)
powder room	huazhuang jian	(hwah-jwahng jee-in)
men's toilet	nan cesuo	(nahn tsuh-swaw)
women's toilet	nu cesuo	(nuu tsuh-swaw)

flush toilet	cong cesuo	(tsoong tsuh-swaw)
toilet paper	shouzhi	(show-jr)

Where is the nearest toilet?
Nali you zuijin-de cesuo?
(Nah-lee yoe zway-jeen-duh tsuh-swaw?)

Is there a toilet on this floor?
Zhe yi ceng you cesuo ma?
(Juh ee tsuung yoe tsuh-swaw mah?)

May I use the toilet?
Wo keyi yong cesuo ma?
(Waw kuh-ee yoong tsuh-swaw mah?)

At the Barber Shop/Beauty Parlor
Barber shop   Lifa guan
(Lee-fah gwahn)

back (of head)	houmian	(hoe-mee-in)
beard	huxu	(huu-shu)
haircut	lifa	(lee-fah)
front	qianmian	(chee-in-mee-in)
little bit	yidian	(ee-dee-in)
long	chang	(chahng)

massage	anmo	(ahn-mwo)
mustache	xiao huzi	(shee-ow huu-dzu)
shave	gualian guahuzi	(gwah-lee-in); (gwah-huu-dzu)
short	duan	(dwahn)
top	ding tou	(deeng); (toe)
sideburns	lianbing huzi	(lee-in-beeng huu-dzu)

I would like a haircut.
Wo yao lifa.
(Waw yow lee-fah.)

Please don't cut it too short.
Qing bie tain duan.
(Cheeng bee-eh tah-een dwahn.)

Just a trim, please.
Qing ba toufa jianqi.
(Cheeng bah toe-fah jee-in-chee.)

Please cut it a little shorter.
Qing jian duan yidian.
(Cheeng jee-in dwahn ee-dee-in.)

Please cut a little more off the top.
Qing zai dingshang zai jian yidian.
(Cheeng zigh deeng-shahng zigh jee-in ee-dee-in.)

I would like a shave.
Wo yao gua lian.
(Waw yow gwah lee-in.)

No shampoo, thank you.
Bu yao xitou, xiexie.
(Buu yow she-toe, she-eh-she-eh.)

Beauty parlor   Meiyong yuan
(May-yoong ywen)

facial massage	mianbu anmo	(mee-in-buu ahn-mwo)
haircut	lifa	(lee-fah)
hairspray	jiaoshui	(jee-ow-shway)
manicure	xiu zhijia	(sheo jr-jee-ah)
permanent	tang toufa	(tahng toe-fah)
shampoo	xitou	(she-toe)
wash, blow dry	xihou chuigan	(she-hoe chway-gahn)

Please give me a _____.
Qing wei wo _____.
(Cheeng way waw _____.)

Signs in China

admission free	mianfei ruchang	(mee-in-fay ruu-chahng)
arrivals	jinguan	(jeen-gwahn)

216

bathroom	yushi	(yuu-shr)
bicycle parking	cunche chu	(tswun-chuh chuu)
car parking lot	tingche chang	(teeng-chuh chahng)
business hours	yingye shijian	(eeng-yeh shr-jee-in)
bus stop	qiche zhan	(chee-chuh jahn)
caution	xiaoxin	(shee-ow-sheen)
closed (business)	tingzhiyingye	(teeng-jr-eeng-yeh);
	guanmen	(gwahn-mun)
customs	haiguan	(high-gwahn)
danger	weixian	(way-shee-in)
departures	chuguan	(chuu-gwahn)
dismount at gate (bicyclists)	churu qing xia che	(chuu-ruu cheeng she-ah chuh)
do not enter	buxu jinru	(buu-shu jeen-ruu)
don't touch	wuchu wumo	(wuu-chuu); (wuu-mwo)

drinking water	yingyong shui	(eeng-yoong shway)
elevator	dianti	(dee-in-tee)
emergency exit	jinji chukou taiping men	(jeen-jee chuu-koe); (tie-peeng mun)
employees only	xianren mianru	(shee-in-wren mee-in-ruu)
engaged (toilet)	shiyongzhong	(shr-yoong-joong)
entrance	rukou	(ruu-koe)
exit	chukou	(chuu-koe)
first aid	jijiu	(jee-jew)
forbidden	jinzhi	(jeen-jr)
for rent	chuzu	(chuu-zuu)
hospital	yiyuan	(ee-ywen)
information	tongzhi	(toong-jr)
information desk	xunwen chu	(shwun-wun chuu)
information office	wenxun chu	(wun-shwun chuu)

keep off lawn	qing wu jianta caoping	(cheeng wuu jee-in-tah tsow-peeng)
keep out	qie wu runei	(chee-eh wuu ruu-nay)
ladies' room	nu cesuo	(nuu tsuh-swaw)
left luggage storage	xingli jicun chu	(sheeng-lee jee-tswun chuu)
luggage lockers	xingli gui	(sheeng-lee gway)
men's room	nan cesuo	(nahn tsuh-swaw)
nonpotable water	fei yinyong shui	(fay eeng-yoong shway)
no entrance	jinzhi runei	(jeen-jr ruu-nay)
no entry	qinzhi runei	(cheen-jr ruu-nay)
no parking	bu xutingche	(buu shu-teeng-chuh)
no picture-taking	qing wu pai-zhao	(cheeng wuu pie-jow)
no smoking, please	qing wu ziyan	(cheeng wuu dzu-yahn)

no spitting, please	qing wu tutan	(cheeng wuu tuu-tahn)
no trespassing	buzhun runei	(buu-juwun ruu-nay)
open (for business)	yingye	(eeng-yeh)
platform	yuetie	(yu-eh-tee-eh)
please don't touch	qing wu dongshou	(cheeng wuu doong-show)
please do not touch exhibits	qing wu chumo zhanpin	(cheeng wuu chuu-mwo jahn-peen)
please queue	qing paidui	(cheeng pie-dway)
police	jingchahu	(jeeng-chah-huu)
public bath	yu chi	(yuu chee)
public telephone	gongyong dianhua	(goong-yoong dee-in-hwah)
public toilet	gongyong cesuo	(goong-yoong tsuh-swaw)
pull	la	(lah)

push	tui	(tway)
reserved	yuyue	(yuu-yu-eh)
self-service	zizhu	(dzu-juu)
smoking permitted	keyi xiyan	(kuh-ee she-yahn)
sold out, full house	quanman ke man	(chwahn-mahn); (kuh mahn)
ticket office	shoupiao chu	(show-pee-ow chuu)
toilet	cesuo	(tsuh-swaw)
vacancy	you kong fang	(yoe koong fahng)
waiting room	xiuxi shi	(sheo-she shr)

Colors

black	hei	(hay)
blue	lan	(lahn)
brown	zong	(zoong)
gray	hui	(hway)

green	lu	(luu)
red	hong	(hoong)
white	bai	(buy)
yellow	huang	(hwahng)

Measurements

China uses the metric system.

millimeter	haomi	(how-me)
centimeter	limi	(lee-me)
meter	mi	(me)
kilometer	gongli	(goong-lee)
milligram	haoke	(how-kuh)
gram	gongke	(goong-kuh)
kilogram	gongjin	(goong-jeen)
metric ton	gongdun	(goong-dwun)
milliliter	haosheng	(how-shuung)
liter	sheng	(shuung)
hectare (2.47 acres)	gongqing	(goong-cheeng)

Making up Your Own Sentences
Occupations/Titles

profession   zhiye   (jr-yeh)

What is your profession?
Shenme shi ni-de zhi ye?
(Shuun-muh shr nee-duh jr-yeh?)

I am a/an _____.
Wo shi _____.
(Waw shr _____.)

Academic titles

chancellor, president	xiaozhang	(shee-ow-jahng)
department chairperson	xi zhuren	(she juu-wren)
group head (study)	jiaoyanshi zhuren	(jee-ow-yahn-shr juu-wren)
professor	jiaoshou	(jee-ow-show)

Business/Professional titles

actor	nanyanyuan	(nahn-yahn-ywen)
actress	nuyanyuan	(nuu-yahn-ywen)
accountant	kuaijiyuan	(kwie-jee-ywen)

artist	huajia	(hwah-jee-ah)
attorney	lushi	(luu-shr)
banker	yinhangjia	(een-hahng-jee-ah)
businessperson	shangren	(shahng-wren)
chairperson	zhuxi	(juu-she)
computer specialist	diannao zhuanjia	(dee-in-now jwahn-jee-ah)
consultant	guwen	(guu-wun)
doctor	yisheng	(ee-shuung)
driver	siji	(suh-jee)
editor	bianji	(bee-in-jee)
engineer	gongchengshi	(goong-chuung-shr)
engineer-in-chief	zong gongchengshi	(zoong-goong-chuung-shr)
entertainer	biaoyanzhe	(bee-ow-yahn-juh)
factory manager/ director	changzhang	(chahng-jahng)

farmer	nongfu	(noong-fuu)
foreman (workshop)	chejian zhuren	(chuh-jee-in juu-wren)
general (army)	jiangjun	(jee-ahng-jwin)
general manager	zong jingli	(zoong jeeng-lee)
journalist	jizhe	(jee-juh)
government official	guan	(gwahn)
government employee	ganbu	(gahn-buu)
guide	daoyou	(dow-yoe)
laborer	gongren	(goong-wren)
lawyer	lushi	(luu-shr)
librarian	tushuguanliyuan	(tuu-shuu-gwahn-lee-ywen)
manager	jingli	(jeeng-lee)
mechanic	jigong	(jee-goong)
musician	yinyuejia	(een-yu-eh-jee-ah)

minister, preacher	mushi	(muu-shr)
nurse	hushi	(huu-shr)
office worker	zhiyuan	(jr-ywen)
Ph.D., Dr.	boshi	(bwo-shr)
photographer	sheyingshi	(shuh-eeng-shr)
priest	shenfu	(shuun-fuu)
professor	jiaoshou	(jee-ow-show)
scientist	kexuejia	(kuh-shu-eh-jee-ah)
secretary	mishu	(me-shuu)
sportsperson	yundongyuan	(ywun-doong-ywen)
student	xuesheng	(shu-eh-shuung)
teacher	laoshi	(lou-shr)
technician	jishuyuan	(jee-shuu-ywen)
tourist	luke	(luu-kuh)

translator	fanyi	(fahn-ee)
travel agent	luxing yuan	(luu-sheeng ywen)
writer	zuojia	(zwaw-jee-ah)

I am a student.
Wo shi xuesheng.
(Waw shr shu-eh-shuung.)

Here is my student identification card.
Zhe shi wo-de xuesheng zheng.
(Juh shr waw-duh shu-eh-shuung juung.)

Government titles

cadre (government staff)	ganbu	(gahn-buu)
director of bureau	juzhang	(juu-jahng)
director of department	sizhang	(suh-jahng)
director of subdepartment	chuzhang	(chuu-jahng)
governor	shengzhang	(shuung-jahng)
mayor	shizhang	(shr-jahng)
minister	buzhang	(buu-jahng)
vice-minister	fu buzhang	(fuu buu-jahng)

premier	zongli	(zoong-lee)
vice-premier	fu zongli	(fuu zoong-lee)
president	zongtong	(zoong-toong)
vice-president	fu zongtong	(fuu zoong-toong)

Where is (the) _____?
_____ zai nali?
(_____ zigh nah-lee?)

American Consulate	Meiguo Lingshiguan	(May-gwaw Leeng-shr-gwahn)
American Embassy	Meiguo Dashiguan	(May-gwaw Dah-shr-gwahn)
bank	yinhang	(een-hahng)
barber shop	lifa dian	(lee-fah dee-in)
bicycle shop	zixingche dian	(dzu-sheeng-chuh dee-in)
bookstore	shu dian	(shuu dee-in)
bus station	gonggongqiche zhan	(goong-goong-chee-chuh jahn)

bus stop	qiche zhan	(chee-chuh jahn)
dining car	can che	(tsahn chuh)
dining room	can ting	(tsahn teeng)
entrance	rukou	(ruu-koe)
exit	chukou	(chuu-koe)
Friendship Store	Youyishang Dian	(Yoe-ee-shahng Dee-in)
hospital	yiyuan	(ee-ywen)
hotel	luguan	(luu-gwahn)
information office	wenxun chu	(wun-shwun chuu)
library	tushuguan	(tuu-shuu-gwahn)
police station	jingcha ju	(jeeng-chah juu)
post office	you ju	(yoe juu)
reception desk	fuwu tai	(fuu-wuu tie)
restaurant	fanguan	(fahn-gwahn)
subway station	ditie zhan	(dee-tee-eh jahn)
swimming pool	youyong chi	(yoe-yoong chee)

taxi stand	chuzu qiche zhan	(chuu-zuu chee-chuh jahn)
telephone	dianhua	(dee-in-hwah)
tennis court	wangqiu chang	(wahng-cheo-chahng)
ticket office	shoupiao chu	(show-pee-ow chuu)
toilet	cesuo	(tsuh-swaw)
tourist bus	youlan che	(yoe-lahn chuh)

I need _____.
Wo xuyao _____.
(Waw shu-yow _____.)

I would like _____.
Wo xiang yao _____.
(Waw shee-ahng yow _____.)

We would like _____.
Women xiang yao.
(Waw-mun shee-ahng yow _____.)

I want _____.
Wo yao _____.
(Waw yow _____.)

I want to go to _____.
Wo yao qu _____.
(Waw yow chu _____.)

Let's go to _____.
Women dao _____ qu.
(Waw-mun dow _____ chu.)

I'm looking for _____.
Wo zai zhao _____.
(Waw zigh jow _____.)

Please give me _____.
Qing gei wo _____.
(Cheeng gay waw _____.)

Please bring me _____.
Qing songlai wo _____.
(Cheeng soong-lie waw _____.)

Please take me to _____.
Qing dai wo dao _____.
(Cheeng die waw dow _____.)

Please pick me up at _____.
Qing _____ jie wo.
(Cheeng _____ jee-eh waw.)

Please come back at _____.
Qing hui lai _____.
(Cheeng hwee lie.)

I will return at _____.
Wo _____ hui lai _____.
(Waw _____ hwee lie _____.)

I will meet you at _____.
Wo _____ jian ni.
(Waw _____ jee-in nee.)

Do you have (any) _____?
Is there (a/any) _____?
Youmei you _____?
(Yoe-may yoe _____?)

I would like to buy _____.
Wo yao mai _____.
(Waw yow my _____.)

I would like some _____.
Wo yao _____.
(Waw yow _____.)

Please show me _____.
Qing gei wo kan _____.
(Cheeng gay waw kahn _____.)

Excuse me, where is the nearest _____?
Qing wen, zuijinde _____ zai nar?
(Cheeng wun, zway-jeen-duh _____ zigh nah-urr?)

Public Holidays and Festivals

January 1:
New Year's Day
Yuan Dan
(Yuu-ahn Dahn)

Late January/early February:
Spring Festival
Chun Jie
(Chwun Jee-eh)*

End of February:
Lantern Festival
Yuanxiao Jie
(Ywen-shee-ow Jee-eh)

March 8:
International Women's Day
San Ba Funu Jie
(Sahn Bah Fuu-nuu Jee-eh)

Early April:
Pure Brighteness Festival
Qingming Jie
(Cheeng-meeng Jee-eh)

May 1:
National Labor Day
Guoji Laodong Jie
(Gwaw-jee Lou-doong Jee-eh)

Late May/early June:
Dragon Boat Festival
Duan Wu Jie
(Dwahn Wuu Jee-eh)

---

* This is the Chinese equivalent of the New Year's celebration.

June 1:
Children's Day
Liuyi Ertong Jie
(Leo-ee Urr-toong Jee-eh)

Early September:
Moon Festival
Zhongqiu Jie
(Joong-cheo Jee-eh)

October 1:
National Celebration Day
Guo Qing Jie
(Gwaw Cheeng Jee-eh)

PART THREE

General Vocabulary

A

abacus	suanpan	(swahn-pahn)
abortion	liuchan	(leo-chahn)
about	dayue chabuduo	(dah-yu-eh); (chah-buu- dwaw)
abroad	guowai	(gwaw-wigh)
accept	shou jieshou	(show); (jee-eh-show)
accident	shigu yiwai	(shr-guu); (ee-wigh)
accurate	zhunque	(juwun-chu-uh)
achievement	chengguo	(chuung-gwaw)
acid rain	suan yu	(swahn yuu)
actor	yanyuan	(yahn-ywen)
acupuncture	zhenjiu	(jun-jeo)
adaptor plug	zhuanjie chatou	(jwahn-jee-eh chah-toe)
address	dizhi zhuzhi	(dee-jr); (juu-jr)
address book	tongxun bu	(toong-shwun buu)
addressee	duifang	(dway-fahng)
admission	ruchang	(ruu-chahng)
adult	daren	(dah-wren)

aerobics	jianmei cao	(jee-in-may tsow)
a few	jige	(jee-guh)
afraid	pa	(pah)
after	guo	(gwaw)
afternoon	xiawu	(shee-ah-wuu)
again	zai	(zigh)
against	dui	(dway)
age	nianling sui	(nee-in-leeng); (sway)
agree	tongyi	(toong-ee)
agriculture	nongye	(noong-yeh)
AIDS	aizi bing	(eye-dzu beeng)
air	kongqi	(koong-chee)
air-conditioned	kongtiao	(koong-tee-ow)
air conditioner	kongtiaoji	(koong-tee-ow-jee)
airline (company)	hangkong gongsi	(hahng-koong goong-suh)
airline hostess	kongzhong xiaojie	(koong-joong shee-ow-jee-eh)
airmail	hangkong youjian	(hahng-koong yoe-jee-in)
airmail stamp	hangkong youpiao	(hahng-koong yoe-pee-ow)
airplane	feiji	(fay-jee)

airplane ticket	feiji piao	(fay-jee pee-ow)
air pollution	kongqi wuran	(koong-chee wuu-rahn)
airport	feijichang	(fay-jee-chahng)
airsick	yunji	(ywun-jee)
alarm clock	nao zhong	(now joong)
alcohol	jiu	(jeo)
a little	yidian	(ee-dee-in)
all	dou	(doe)
allergic	goumin	(gwaw-meen)
allergy	goumin	(gwaw-meen)
alley	hutong	(huu-toong)
altitude	haiba	(high-bah)
ambassador	dashi	(dah-shr)
amount, sum, total	jin e	(jeen uh)
amusing, fun	haowanr	(how-wahn-urr)
ancient	gudai-de	(guu-die-duh)
angry	shengqi	(shuung-chee)
animal	dongwu	(doong-wuu)
anniversary	zhounian jinian	(joe-nee-in jee-nee-in)
announcement	diantai huo	(dee-in-tie hwaw)
answer	huida	(hway-dah)
antibiotics	kangshengsu	(kahng-shuung-suu)

antique	guwan gudong	(guu-wahn); (guu-doong)
antique store	gudong dian	(guu-doong dee-in)
apartment	danyuan fang	(dahn-ywen fahng)
appendicitis	lanweiyan	(lahn-way-yahn)
appetite	shiyu weikou	(shr-yuu); (way-koe)
appetizer	lengpan	(luung-pahn)
applaud	paishou	(pie-show)
appliance	dianqi	(dee-in-chee)
application	shengqing	(shuung-cheeng)
application form	shengqing biao	(shuung-cheeng bee-ow)
appointment	yuehui	(yu-eh-hway)
appreciate	xinshang	(sheen-shahng)
approve	pizhun	(pee-juwun)
archaeology	kaoguxue	(kow-guu-shu- eh)
architecture	jianzhuxue	(jee-in-juu-shu- eh)
area (district)	yidai	(ee-die)
army	jundui	(jwin-dway)
arrangement	anpai	(ahn-pie)
arrive	daoda	(dow-dah)
art	yishu meishu	(ee-shuu); (may-shuu)

art gallery	hualang	(hwah-lahng)
artist	yishujia	(ee-shuu-jee-ah)
art museum	meishu guan	(may-shuu gwahn)
arts and crafts	gongyi meishu	(goong-ee may-shuu)
Asia	Yazhou	(Yah-joe)
ask	wen	(wun)
aspirin	asipilin	(ah-suh-pee-leen)
assignment	gongzuo	(goong-zwaw)
assist, aid	bangzhu	(bahng-juu)
asthma	qichuanbing	(chee-chwahn-beeng)
athletics	yundong	(ywun-doong)
attorney	lushi	(luu-shr)
attractive	xiyinren-de	(she-een-wren-duh)
audience	guanzhong	(gwahn-joong)
auditorium	litang	(lee-tahng)
aunt	gugu	(guu-guu)
authentic	kekao-de	(kuh-kow-duh)
author	zuozhe	(zwaw-juh)
authorize	shouchuan	(show-chwahn)
automatic	zidong-de	(dzu-doong-duh)
automobile	qiche	(chee-chuh)
avenue	dajie	(dah-jee-eh)

average	pingjun	(peeng-jwin)
awake, wake up	huanxing	(hwahn-sheeng)

B

baby	yinger	(eeng-urr)
baby food	yinger shipin	(eeng-urr shr-peen)
bachelor	danshenhan	(dahn-shuun-hahn)
back door	hou men	(hoe mun)
back yard	hou yuan	(hoe ywen)
bad quality	cha	(chah)
bag	daizi	(die-dzu)
baggage	xingli	(sheeng-lee)
baggage cart	xingli che	(sheeng-lee chuh)
baggage check	xingli tuoyundan	(sheeng-lee twaw-ywun-dahn)
baggage claim	xingli ting	(sheeng-lee teeng)
baggage tag	xingli pai	(sheeng-lee pie)
bakery	mianbao dian	(mee-in-bow dee-in)

ball	qiu	(cheo)
ball game, match	qiusai	(cheo-sigh)
ballpoint pen	yuanzhu bi	(ywen-juu bee)
ballroom	wuting	(wuu-teeng)
bamboo	zhuzi	(juu-dzu)
bamboo shoots	zhusun	(juu-suun)
banana	xiangjiao	(shee-ahng-jee-ow)
band (musical)	yuedui	(yu-eh-dway)
bandage	bengdai	(buung-die)
band-aid	zhixue jiaobu	(jr-shu-eh jee-ow-buu)
bank	yinhang	(een-hahng)
banquet	yanhui	(yahn-hway)
banquet room	yanhui ting	(yahn-hway teeng)
bar (drinking)	jiuba	(jeo-bah)
barbecue	kao	(kow)
barber shop	lifa dian	(lee-fah dee-in)
barter	yihou yihou	(ee-hoe ee-hoe)
baseball	bangqiu	(bahng-cheo)
basement	dixiashi	(dee-shee-ah-shr)
basketball	lanqiu	(lahn-cheo)
basketball match	lanqiu sai	(lahn-cheo sigh)
bath	yugang	(yuu-gahng)
bathe	xizao	(she-zow)

bathing beach	yu chang	(yuu chahng)
bathing suit	youyongyi	(yoe-yoong-ee)
bathrobe	shuipao	(shway-pow)
bathroom (bath) (toilet)	yushi cesuo	(yuu-shr); (tsuh-swaw)
bath towel	xizao maojin	(she-zow mou-jeen)
bathtub	zaopen	(zow-pin)
batteries	dianchi	(dee-in-chee)
bay	haiwan	(high-wahn)
beach	haitan	(high-tahn)
bean curd	doufu	(doe-fuu)
beard	huzi	(huu-dzu)
beat, win	ying	(eeng)
beautiful	piaoliang-de	(pee-ow-lee-ahng-duh)
beauty, natural	ziranmei	(dzu-rahn-may)
beauty salon	falang	(fah-lahng)
beauty spot	mingsheng	(meeng-shuung)
bed	chuang	(chwahng)
bedbugs	chouchong	(choe-choong)
bedroom	woshi wofang	(waw-shr); (waw-fahng)
bedsheet	chuang dan	(chwahng dahn)
beef	niurou	(neo-roe)
beefsteak	niu pai	(neo pie)
beer	pijiu	(pee-jeo)

before	yiqian	(ee-chee-in)
beggar	qigai	(chee-guy)
behind	zai . . . houbian	(zigh . . . hoe-bee-in)
bell (door)	ling	(leeng)
bell captain	xingli lingban	(sheeng-lee leeng-bahn)
belt	yaodai	(yow-die)
beside, next to	zai . . . pangbian	(zigh . . . pahng-bee-in)
best	zuihao	(zway-how)
better	bijiaohao	(bee-jee-ow-how)
between	zai . . . zhijian	(zigh . . . jr-jee-in)
bicycle	zixingche	(dzu-sheeng-chuh)
big, large, great	da	(dah)
bill (charge; noun)	zhangdan piaoju	(jahng-dahn); (pee-ow-juu)
bill (verb)	kai zhangdan	(kigh jahng-dahn)
bind, tie	kun	(kwun)
birds	niao	(nee-ow)
birth	sheng	(shuung)
birth control	jieyu	(jee-eh-yuu)
birthday (of old person)	shengri shouchen	(shuung-rr); (show-chun)

biscuit	binggan	(beeng-gahn)
bitter	ku de	(kuu duh)
black	hei	(hay)
blanket	tanzi	(tahn-dzu)
bleed	liuxue	(leo-shu-eh)
blister	pao	(pow)
blond	jinfa	(jeen-fah)
blood pressure	xueya	(shu-eh-yah)
blood type	xue xing	(shu-eh sheeng)
blouse	chenyi	(chun-ee)
blue	lan	(lahn)
boarding pass	dengji pai	(duung-jee pie)
boat	chuan	(chwahn)
body (human)	shenti	(shuun-tee)
body temperature	tiwen	(tee-wun)
boil (verb)	zhu	(juu)
boiled egg	zhu jidan	(juu jee-dahn)
boiled water	kai shui	(kigh shway)
bon voyage	fengshun yilu	(fuung-shwun); (ee-luu)
book	shu	(shuu)
bookkeeper	kuaiji	(kwie-jee)
bookshop	shu dian	(shuu dee-in)
booth	ting	(teeng)
boots	xuezi	(shu-eh-dzu)

border	bianjie	(bee-in-jay)
borrow	jie	(jee-eh) (jay)
boss	laoban	(lou-bahn)
bottle	ping	(peeng)
bottle opener	kaipingqi	(kigh-peeng-chee)
boulevard	dadao	(dah-dow)
bowl	wan	(wahn)
box	hezi	(huh-dzu)
boxing	quanji	(chwahn-jee)
boy	nanhair	(nahn-high-urr)
boyfriend	nan pengyou	(nahn puung-yoe)
bra	ruzhao	(ruu-jow)
branch office	fen bu	(fin buu)
brand, trademark	shangbiao paihao	(shahng-bee-ow); (pie-how)
brassiere	xiongzhao	(shee-ong-jow)
bread	mianbao	(mee-in-bow)
breast	fufang	(fuu-fahng)
bride	xinniang	(sheen-nee-ahng)
bridegroom	xinlang	(sheen-lahng)
bridge	qiao	(chee-ow)
brother	xiongdi	(shee-ong-dee)
Buddhism	Fojiao	(Fwo-jee-ow)
Buddhist	Fojiao	(Fwo-jee-ow)

budget	yusuan	(yuu-swahn)
buffet	zizhucan	(dzu-juu-tsahn)
buffet dinner	zizhu wancan	(dzu-juu wahn-tsahn)
buffet lunch	zizhu wucan	(dzu-juu wuu-tsahn)
building	loufang	(low-fahng)
bus	gonggongqiche	(goong-goong-chee-chuh)
business	shangye	(shahng-yeh)
businessperson	shangren	(shahng-wren)
bus stop	qiche zhan	(chee-chuh jahn)
busy	mang	(mahng)
butter	huangyou	(hwahng-yoe)
buy	mai	(my)
by	da	(dah);
	zuo	(zwaw)

C

cabbage	yang baicai	(yahng buy-tsigh)
cabin	kecang	(kuh-tsahng)
cable television	bilu dianshi	(bee-luu dee-in-shr)

cadre	ganbu	(gahn-buu)
cafe	kafeiguan	(kah-fay-gwahn)
cafeteria	shitang	(shr-tahng)
cake	dangao	(dahn-gow)
calculator	jisuanji	(jee-swahn-jee)
calendar (lunar)	rili yinli	(rr-lee); (een-lee)
California	Jiazhou	(Jee-ah-joe)
call, phone	da dianhua	(dah dee-in-hwah)
calligraphy	shufu	(shuu-fuu)
calories	kaluli	(kah-luu-lee)
camera	zhaoxiangji	(jow-shee-ahng-jee)
can, tin, jar	guantou	(gwahn-toe)
canal	yunhe	(ywun-huh)
cancel	zhuxiao	(juu-shee-ow)
cancer	aizheng	(eye-juung)
candle	lazhu	(lah-juu)
candy	tangguo	(tahng-gwaw)
can opener	guantou qizi	(gwahn-toe chee-dzu)
capital (city) (money)	shoudu zijin	(show-duu); (dzu-jeen)
capsule	jiaonang	(jee-ow-nahng)
captain (plane)	jizhang	(jee-jahng)
captain (ship)	chuanzhang	(chwahn-jahng)

248

car	che	(chuh)
carpet	ditan	(dee-tahn)
cash (noun)	xianjin	(shee-in-jeen)
cash a check	duixian	(dway-shee-in)
cashier	caiwu chunayuan	(tsigh-wuu); (chuu-nah-ywen)
cassette tape	cidai	(tsu-die)
casual	suibian	(sway-bee-in)
cat	mao	(mou)
cattle	shengkou	(shuung-koe)
cave, grotto	yandong	(yahn-doong)
Catholic	Tianzhujiao	(Tee-in-juu-jee-ow)
ceiling	tianhuaban	(tee-in-hwah-bahn)
centigrade	sheshi	(shuh-shr)
central	zhongyang	(joong-yahng)
central heating	jizhong gongre	(jee-joong goong-ruh)
ceramics	taoqi	(tou-chee)
cereal	maipian	(my-pee-in)
ceremony	dianli	(dee-in-lee)
certified check	baofu zhipiao	(bow-fuu jr-pee-ow)
chair	yizi	(ee-dzu)
change (money)	lingqian	(leeng-chee-in)
changing money	duihuan	(dway-hwahn)

249

cheap	pianyi	(pee-in-ee)
check	zhipiao	(jr-pee-ow)
check in (airport) (verb) (hotel)	ban chengji shouxu dengji	(bahn chuung-jee show-shu); (duung-jee)
check out (hotel) (verb)	tuifang	(tway-fahng)
cheongsam (dress)	qipao	(chee-pow)
chess	guoji xiangqi	(gwaw-jee shee-ahng-chee)
chest pain	xiongkou teng	(shee-ong-koe tuung)
chicken	ji	(jee)
child	haizi	(high-dzu)
children	haizimen	(high-dzu-mun)
China	Zhongguo	(Joong-gwaw)
Chinese (people)	Zhongren	(Joong-wren)
Chinese ideogram	hanzi	(hahn-dzu)
Chinese language	han yu	(hahn yuu)
chocolate	qiaokeli	(chee-ow-kuh-lee)
chop (noun)	yinzhang	(een-jahng)
chopsticks	kuaizi	(kwie-dzu)
Christmas	Shengdanjie	(Shuung-dahn-jee-eh)
church	jiaotang	(jee-ow-tahng)

city, town	chengshi	(chuung-shr)
city map	chengshi jiaotong tu	(chuung-shr jee-ow-toong tuu)
city tour	youlan shirong	(yoe-lahn shr-roong)
civilization	wenming	(wun-meeng)
class (students)	ban	(bahn)
classmate	tongxue	(toong-shu-eh)
clay figure	ni ren	(nee wren)
clean	ganjing	(gahn-jeeng)
climate	qihou	(chee-hoe)
climb (in/on)	shang	(shahng)
cloakroom	yimaojian	(ee-mou-jee-in)
clock	zhong	(joong)
closing time	guan men	(gwahn mun)
clothing	yifu	(ee-fuu)
cloud	yun	(ywun)
club, recreation	julebu	(juu-luh-buu)
coach, bus	changtuqiche	(chahng-tuu-chee-chuh)
coal	mei	(may)
coastline	haian xian	(high-ahn shee-in)
coat	dayi shangyi	(dah-ee); (shahng-ee)
coat hanger	yijia	(ee-jee-ah)

cockroach	zhanglang	(jahng-lahng)
cocktail	jiweijiu	(jee-way-jeo)
cocktail party	jiweijiuhui	(jee-way-jeo-hway)
coffee	kafei	(kah-fay)
coffee shop	kafei dian	(kah-fay dee-in)
coins	yingbi	(eeng-bee)
cold	leng	(luung)
cold cuts (food)	shushi	(shuu-shr)
cold dishes	lengpan	(luung-pahn)
college, university	daxue	(dah-shuu-eh)
color	yanse	(yahn-suh)
comb	shuzi	(shuu-dzu)
comedy	xiju	(she-juu)
comfortable	shufu	(shuu-fuu)
communication	jiaotong	(jee-ow-toong)
Communist Party	Gongchandang	(Goong-chahn-dahng)
company, firm	gongsi	(goong-suh)
compartment	chexiang	(chuh-shee-ahng)
competition	jingzheng	(jeeng-juung)
computer	diannao	(dee-in-now)
concert	yinyuehui	(een-yu-eh-hway)
condom	yinjingtao	(een-jeeng-tou)

conductor (bus)	shoupianoyuan	(show-pee-in-aw-ywen);
(train)	chengwuyuan	(chuung-wuu-ywen)
conference room	huiyi shi	(hway-ee shr)
Confucius	Kongzi	(Koong-dzu)
confused	kunao	(kuu-now)
congratulations	gongxi	(goong-she)
constipation	bianbi	(bee-in-bee)
consulate	lingshiguan	(leeng-shr-gwahn)
contact lenses	yinxing yanjing	(een-sheeng yahn-jeeng)
contagious	chuanran	(chwahn-rahn)
contraceptive	biyunyao	(bee-ywun-yow)
contract	hetong	(huh-toong)
conversation	huihua	(hway-hwah)
corner (street)	guaijiao	(gwie jee-ow)
correct	dui	(dway);
	zhengque	(juung-chu-uh)
corridor	loudao	(low-dow)
cost	yao	(yow)
cot	xiao chuang	(shee-ow chwahng)
cough	kesou	(kuh-soe)
cough drops	kesou tang	(kuh-soe tahng)
count (noun)	xian	(shee-in)

count (verb)	jishu	(jee-shuu)
counter (sales)	guitai	(gway-tie);
(service)	fuwutai	(fuu-wuu-tie)
country (nation)	guojia	(gwaw-jee-ah)
countryside	nongcun	(noong-tswun)
couple (married)	fufu	(fuu-fuu);
(two)	liang	(lee-ahng)
court	fayuan	(fah-ywen)
courtyard	yuanzi	(ywen-dzu)
cow	niu	(neo)
cramps	choujin	(choe-jeen)
cream	naiyou	(nigh-yoe)
credit card	xinyong ka	(sheen-yoong kah)
crossroads	shizilukou	(shr-dzu-luu-koe)
crowd	renqun	(wren-chwun)
crowded	yongji	(yoong-jee)
cultural	wenhua-de	(wun-hwah-duh)
cultural exchange	wenhua jiaoliu	(wun-hwah jee-ow-leo)
cultural relic	wenhua guji	(wun-hwah guu-jee)
culture	wenhua	(wun-hwah)
cup, glass	beizi	(bay-dzu)
currency	huobi	(hwaw-bee)
curtain	chuanglian	(chwahng-lee-in)

254

custom, way	fengsu xiguan	(fuung-suu); (she-gwahn)
customer	guke	(guu-kuh)
Customs	Haiguan	(High-gwahn)
customs law	haiguan fa	(high-gwahn fah)
customs tariff	guanshui shuize	(gwahn-shway shway-zuh)

dad	baba	(bah-bah)
daily	meitian	(may-tee-in)
daily paper	ri bao	(rr bow)
dairy	niunai dian	(neo-nigh dee-in)
dance (verb)	tiaowu	(tee-ow-wuu)
dance hall	wu ting	(wuu teeng)
dance party	wu hui	(wuu hway)
dangerous	weixiande	(way-shee-in- duh)
dark	ande	(ahn-duh)
date (period) (meeting) (courting)	riqi yuehui tan lian ai	(rr-chee); (yu-eh-hway); (tahn lee-in eye)
daughter	nuer	(nuu-urr)

daughter-in-law	er-xi-fu	(urr-she-fuu)
dawn	liming	(lee-meeng)
day	tian	(tee-in)
daytime	baitian	(buy-tee-in)
deep	shen	(shuun)
degree (college)	xuewei	(shu-eh-way)
delay	yanhuan	(yahn-hwahn)
delegation	daibiaotuan	(die-bee-ow-twahn)
delicatessen	shushi dian	(shuu-shr dee-in)
delicious	haochi	(how-chee)
deliver	song	(soong)
democracy	minzhu	(meen-juu)
demonstration	shiwei	(shr-way)
dentist	yayi	(yah-ee)
dentures	jiaya	(jee-ah-yah)
deny	jujue	(juu-ju-eh)
deodorant	chuhanji	(chuu-hahn-jee)
department	bu	(buu)
department store	baihuo dian	(buy-hwaw dee-in)
departure	chufa	(chuu-fah)
deposit (money)	yajin	(yah-jeen)
desert	shamo	(shah-mwo)
desk	shuzhuo	(shuu-jwaw)
dessert	tianpin	(tee-in peen)

develop (film)	chongxi	(choong-she)
diabetes	tangniaobing	(tahng-nee-ow-beeng)
diaper	zhiniaobu	(jr-nee-ow-buu)
diarrhoea	fuxie	(fuu-she-eh)
dictionary	zidian	(dzu-dee-in)
different	butong	(buu-toong)
difficult	nan	(nahn)
dining car	canche	(tsahn-chuh)
dining room	canting	(tsahn-teeng)
dinner	wanfan	(wahn-fahn)
direction	fangxiang	(fahng-shee-ahng)
diplomat	waijiaojia	(wigh-jee-ow-jee-ah);
	waijiaorenyuan	(wigh-jee-ow-wren-ywen)
dirty	zang	(zahng)
disabled person	canfei ren	(tsahn-fay wren)
disaster	zainan	(zigh-nahn)
disco	diske	(dees-kuh)
discount	zhekou	(juh-koe)
disembark	xia	(shee-ah)
dish, plate	panzi	(pahn-dzu)
disinfectant	xiaoduji	(shee-ow-duu-jee)
dissatisfied	bumanyi	(buu-mahn-ee)

disturb	darao	(dah-rou)
divorce	lihun	(lee-hwun)
dock	matou	(mah-toe)
doctor	yisheng	(ee-shuung)
documentary (film)	jilu pian	(jee-luu pee-in)
dog	gou	(go)
doll	wawa	(wah-wah)
dollar	meiyuan	(may-ywen)
domestic	guonei	(gwaw-nay)
donkey	lu	(luu)
door, gate	men	(mun)
doorbell	menling	(mun-leeng)
doorway	menkou	(mun-koe)
dormitory	sushe	(suu-shuh)
double bed	shuangren chuang	(shwahng-wren chwahng)
double room	shuangren fang	(shwahng-wren fahng)
downstairs	louxia	(low-shee-ah)
downtown	shizhongxin	(shr-joong-sheen)
dozen	da	(dah)
dragon	long	(loong)
Dragon Boat Festival	Duan Wu Jie	(Dwahn Wuu Jee-eh)

dragon boat race	long zhou bisai	(loong joe bee-sigh)
dress (noun)	yifu	(ee-fuu)
dress (verb)	chuan	(chwahn)
drink (noun)	yinliao	(een-lee-ow)
drink (verb)	he	(huh)
drinking straw	xiguanr	(she-gwahn-urr)
drive (car)	kai	(kigh)
driver	siji	(suh-jee)
driver's license	jiashi zhishao	(jee-ah-shr jr-shou)
drizzle (rain)	maomaoyu	(mou-mou-yuu)
drop, lose	diudiao	(deo-dee-ow)
drug	dupin	(duu-peen)
drugstore	yaodian	(yow dee-in)
drunk, tipsy	zui	(zway)
dry	gan	(gahn)
dry-clean	gan xi	(gahn-she)
dry cleaner's	gan xi dian	(gahn she dee-in)
duck	ya	(yah)
due	daoqi	(dow-chee)
dull, dim, dark	an	(ahn)
dust (noun)	huichen	(hway-chun)
dusty	huichenduo	(hway-chun-dwaw)

| duty (customs) | shui | (shway) |
| duty free | mianshui | (mee-in shway) |

E

each	mei, mei-ge	(may, may-guh)
ear	erduo	(urr-dwaw)
earache	erduo tang	(urr-dwaw tahng)
early	zao	(zow)
earphone	erji	(urr-jee)
earring	erhuan	(urr-hwahn)
earth (planet)	diqiu	(dee-cheo)
earthquake	dizhen	(dee-jun)
east	dong	(doong)
East China Sea	Dong Hai	(Doong High)
east side	dong bian	(doong bee-in)
easy	rongyi	(roong-ee)
eat	chi	(chee)
eat a meal	chifan	(chee-fahn)
economy	jingji	(jeeng-jee)
editor	bianji	(bee-in-jee)
education	jiaoyu	(jee-ow-yuu)
eel	manyu	(mahn-yuu)

egg	jidan	(jee-dahn)
eggplant	qiezi	(chee-eh-dzu)
election	xuanju	(shwen-juu)
electrical goods	dianqi pin	(dee-in-chee peen)
electric fan	dian fengshan	(dee-in fuung-shahn)
electric heater	dian reqi	(dee-in ruh-chee)
electrician	dianggong	(dee-in-goong)
electricity	dian	(dee-in)
electric light	dian deng	(dee-in duung)
electric plug	dian chatou	(dee-in chah-toe)
elephant	xiang	(shee-ahng)
elevator	dianti	(dee-in-tee)
embassy	dashiguan	(dah-shr-gwahn)
emergency	jinjishijian	(jeen-jee-shr-jee-in)
emergency door	taiping men	(tie-peeng mun)
emergency room	jizhen shi	(jee-jun shr)
employee	gongzuoren-yuan	(goong-zwaw-wren-ywen)
empty	kong-de	(koong-duh)
endorse	beishu	(bay-shuu)
energy	nengliang	(nung-lee-ahng)
engineer	gongchengshi	(goong-chuung-shr)

England	Yingguo	(Eeng-gwaw)
English language	Yingwen	(Eeng-wun)
enjoy oneself	guo-de yukai	(gwaw-duh yuu-kigh)
enter	zoujin	(zoe-jeen)
enterprise	qiye	(chee-yeh)
entertain guests	dai ke	(die kuh)
entire, whole	zhengge	(juung-guh)
entrance	rukou	(ruu-koe)
entry visa	rujing qianzheng	(ruu-jeeng chee-in-juung)
envelope	xinfeng	(sheen-fung)
environment	huanjing	(hwahn-jeeng)
equator	chidao	(chee-dow)
error	cuowu	(tswaw-wuu)
escalator	zidongfuti	(dzu-doong-fuu-tee)
Europe	Ouzhou	(Oh-joe)
European (person)	Ouzhouren	(Oh-joe-wren)
evening	wanshang	(wahn-shahng)
evening dress	wan lifu	(wahn lee-fuu)
evening party	wan hui	(wahn hway)
everyday	tiantian	(tee-in-tee-in)
example	lizi	(lee-dzu)
exchange rate	duihuanlu	(dway-hwahn-luu)

exhausted	leihuai-le	(lay-hwie-luh)
exhibition	zhanlanhui	(jahn-lahn-hway)
exhibition hall	zhanlan guan	(jahn-lahn gwahn)
exit	chukou	(chuu-koe)
exit visa	chujing qianzheng	(chuu-jeeng chee-in-juung)
expenses	feiyong	(fay-yoong)
expensive	gui	(gway)
expert	shulian-de	(shuu-lee-in-duh);
	neihang	(nay-hahng)
export	chukou shuchu	(chuu-koe); (shuu-chuu)
export duty	chukou shui	(chuu-koe shway)
export license	chukou xuke zheng	(chuu-koe shu-kuh juung)
express letter	kuaidi	(kwie-dee)
express train	tekudi	(tuh-kuu-dee)
extension cord	jiechang dianxian	(jee-eh-chahng dee-in-shee-in)
extension phone	fenji	(fun-jee)
eye	yan	(yahn)
eyedrops	yanyaoshui	(yahn-yow-shway)
eyeglasses	yanjing	(yahn-jeeng)

face	lian	(lee-in)
fact	shishi	(shr-shr)
factory	gongchang	(goong-chahng)
Fahrenheit	Huashi	(Hwah-shr)
fail	shibai	(shr-buy)
faint	touhun	(toe-hwun)
fake	maopai	(mou-pie)
fall (verb)	shuiaidao	(shway-eye-dow)
false	jiade	(jee-ah-duh)
family	jia	(jee-ah)
family members	qin ren	(cheen wren)
family system	jia pu	(jee-ah puu)
famine	jihuang	(jee-hwahng)
famous	youming	(yoe-meeng)
famous dish	ming cai	(meeng tsigh)
fan (electric)	dian shan	(dee-in shahn)
far	yuan	(ywen)
fare (bus or taxi)	chefei	(chuh-fay)
farm	nongchang	(noong-chahng)
farmer	nongfu	(noong-fuu)
fast	kuai	(kwie)
fast food	kuai can	(kwie tsahn)

fashion	shimao	(shr-mou)
fat	pang	(pahng)
father	fuqin	(fuu-cheen)
faucet	shuilongtou	(shway-loong-toe)
fault	cuo	(tswaw)
fax	chuanzhen	(chwahn-jun)
fee, expense	feiyong	(fay-yoong)
female	nu	(nuu)
ferry	duchuan	(duu-chwahn)
festival	jieri	(jee-eh-rr)
fever	fashao	(fah-shou)
few	shiwu	(shr-wuu)
fiancé	weihunfu	(way-hwun-fuu)
fiancée	weihunqi	(way-hwun-chee)
fiction (book)	xiaoshuo	(shee-ow-shwaw)
field	tiandi	(tee-in-dee)
fight	zhandou	(jahn-doe)
fill in a form	tianxie	(tee-in-she-eh)
film (camera) (movie)	jiaojuan dianying	(jee-ow-jwen); (dee-in-eeng)
film festival	dianying jie	(dee-in-eeng jee-eh)
fine, penalty	fakuan	(fah-kwahn)
finger	shouzhi	(show-jr)
fire	huozai	(hwaw-zigh)

fire alarm	huo jing	(hwaw jeeng)
fire escape	anquan ti	(ahn-chwahn tee)
fire exit	taiping men	(tie-peeng mun)
firecracker	bianpao	(bee-in-pow)
first-aid kit	ji jiu xiang	(jee jeo shee-ahng)
first class	tou deng	(toe duung)
fish	yu	(yuu)
fisherman	yumin	(yuu-meen)
fishing boat	yuchuan	(yuu-chwahn)
fish store	yu dian	(yuu dee-in)
flag	qizi	(chee-dzu)
flash (camera)	shanguangdeng	(shahn-gwahng-duung)
flashlight	shoudiantong	(show-dee-in-toong)
flood	shuizai	(shway-zigh)
floor	lou	(low)
flower	huar	(hwah-urr)
flower shop	huar dian	(hwah-urr dee-in)
flu	ganmao	(gahn-mou)
fly (insect)	cangying	(tsahng-eeng)
fly (verb)	fei	(fay)
fog	wu	(wuu)

foggy	xiawu	(shee-ah-wuu)
folk dance	minjian wudao	(meen-jee-in wuu-dow)
folk music	minjian yinyue	(meen-jee-in een-yu-eh)
food	shiwu	(shr-wuu)
food poisoning	shiwu zhongdu	(shr-wuu joong-duu)
foot (body)	jiao	(jee-ow)
football (U.S.)	ganlanqiu	(gahn-lahn-cheo)
football (soccer)	zuqiu	(zuu-cheo)
forecast	yubao	(yuu-bow)
foreign	waiguo-de	(wigh-gwaw-duh)
foreign exchange	waihui	(wigh-hway)
Foreign Exchange Certificate	Wai Hui Quan	(Wigh Hway Chwahn)
foreign expert	waiguo zhuanjia	(wigh-gwaw jwahn-jee-ah)
foreign guest	waibin	(wigh-been)
forest	shulin senlin	(shuu-leen); (sin-leen)
forget	wang	(wahng)
fork	chazi	(chah-dzu)
form (printed)	biaoge	(bee-ow-guh)
fountain	quan	(chwahn)
France	Faguo	(fah-gwaw)

free (cost)	mianfei	(mee-in-fay);
(time)	you kong	(yoe koong);
(vacant)	meiren	(may-wren)
freelancer	ziyou zhiye zhe	(dzu-yoe jr-yeh juh)
free trade zone	ziyou maoyiqu	(dzu-yoe mou-ee-chu)
freezing	bingdong	(beeng-doong)
French language	Fawen	(Fah-wun)
fresh	xinxian	(sheen-shee-in)
friend	pengyou	(puung-yoe)
Friendship Store	Youyi Shang Dian	(Yoe-ee-Shahng Dee-in)
frog	qingwa	(cheeng-wah)
from	cong	(tsoong)
frost	shuang	(shwahng)
frozen food	lengcang shipin	(luung-tsahng shr-peen)
fruit	shuiguo	(shway-gwaw)
fruit juice	guozhi	(gwaw-jr)
fruit store	shuiguo dian	(shway-gwaw dee-in)
full	man-le	(mahn-luh)
full stomach	bao	(bow)
furniture	jiaju	(jee-ah-juu)
fuse (noun)	baoxiansi	(bow-shee-in-suh)
future	jianglai	(jee-ahng-lie)

G

gallon	jialun	(jee-ah-lwun)
gamble	dubuo	(duu-bwaw)
gambling house	du chang	(duu chahng)
game	youxi	(yoe-she)
game, match	qiusai	(cheo-sigh)
gangway	guodao	(gwaw-dow)
garage	chefang	(chuh-fahng)
garbage	laji	(lah-jee)
garden	huayuan	(hwah-ywen)
garlic	suan	(swahn)
gasoline	qiyou	(chee-yoe)
gas station	jiayou zhan	(jee-ah-yoe jahn)
gate	men	(mun)
genuine	zhende	(jun-duh)
German	Dewen	(duh-wun)
Germany	Deguo	(duh-gwaw)
get on	shang	(shahng)
gift	liwu	(lee-wuu)
ginger	jiang	(jee-ahng)
ginseng	renshen	(wren-shuun)
girl	nuhaizi	(nuu-high-dzu)
girlfriend	nupengyou	(nuu-puung-yoe)

give	gei	(gay)
glass	beizi	(bay-dzu)
glasses (eye)	yanjing	(yahn-jeeng)
gloves	shoutao	(show-tou)
goat	shanyang	(shahn-yahng)
gold	jin	(jeen)
goldfish	jin yu	(jeen yuu)
golf	gaoerfuqiu	(gow-urr-fuu-cheo)
goose	e	(uh)
government	zhengfu	(jung-fuu)
government office	jiguan	(jee-gwahn)
gram	ke	(kuh)
grammar	yufa	(yuu-fah)
Grand Canal	Da Yunhe	(Dah Ywun-huh)
grandfather	zufu	(zuu-fuu)
grandmother	zumu	(zuu-muu)
grandparents	zufumu	(zuu-fuu-muu)
grape juice	putao zhi	(puu-tou jr)
grapes	putao	(puu-tou)
grass	cao	(tsow)
greasy	youwu-de	(yoe-wuu-duh)
great, big	da	(dah)
Great Wall	Chang Cheng	(Chahng Chuung)

green tea	lu cha	(luu chah)
grill food	kaoroujia	(kow-roe-jee-ah)
grocery store	shipin dian	(shr-peen dee-in)
ground, dirt	tudi	(tuu-dee)
ground meat	roumo	(roe-mwo)
group	tuanti	(twahn-tee)
guarantee	baozheng	(bow-juung)
guest	keren	(kuh-wren)
guest house	binguan	(bin-gwahn)
guide	daoyou	(dow-yoe)
guidebook	luyou zhinan	(luu-yoe jr-nahn)
gymnasium	tiyuguan	(tee-yuu-gwahn)
gymnastics	ticao	(tee-tsow)
gynecologist	fukeyisheng	(fuu-kuh-ee-shuung)

H

habit	xiguan	(she-gwahn)
hair	toufa	(toe-fah)
haircut	lifa	(lee-fah)
hairdresser	lifa dian	(lee-fah dee-in)
half	ban	(bahn)

hall, meeting	guan	(gwahn)
ham	houtui	(hoe-tway)
hand	shou	(show)
handbag	shoutibao	(show-tee-bow)
handball	shouqiu	(show-cheo)
handicapped person	canji ren	(tsahn-jee wren)
handicraft	shougongyi pin	(show-goong-ee peen)
handkerchief	shoupa	(show-pah)
handmade	shou-gongzhi-de	(show-goong-jr-duh)
handsome	yingjun	(eeng-jwin)
hand towel	xiao maojin	(shee-ow mou-jeen)
hanger	yijia	(ee-jee-ah)
Happy Birthday	Bai Shou	(Buy Show)
harbor	gangwan	(gahng-wahn)
harvest	shouhou	(show-hoe)
hat	maozi	(mou-dzu)
have	you	(yoe)
have to	yinggai	(eeng-guy)
hay fever	huafen re	(hwah-fin ruh)
he	ta	(tah)
head	tou	(toe)
headache	touteng	(toe-tuung)
health, healthy	jiankang	(jee-in-kahng)

health club	jianshen fang	(jee-in-shuun fahng)
heart	xinzang	(sheen-zahng)
heart attack	xinzangbing fazuo	(sheen-zahng-beeng fah-zwaw)
heater, heating	nuanqi	(nwahn-chee)
heavy	zhong	(joong)
hello (on phone)	wei	(way)
her	ta	(tah)
here	zher	(juhr)
high, tall	gao	(gow)
high-heeled shoes	gao-gen xie	(gow-gun she-eh)
high school	zhong xue	(joong shu-eh)
highway	gonglu	(goong-luu)
hike	jianxing	(jee-in-sheeng)
hill	xiaoshan	(shee-ow-shahn)
him	ta	(tah)
hire, rent	zu	(zuu)
his	ta-de	(tah-duh)
history	lishi	(lee-shr)
hitchhike	dache	(dah-chuh)
hobby	aihao	(eye-how)
holiday	jiaqi jieri	(jee-ah-chee); (jee-eh-rr)

home	jia jiali	(jee-ah, jah); (jee-ah-lee)
home place	jia xiang	(jee-ah shee-ahng)
homesick	xiangjia	(shee-ahng-jee- ah)
hometown	guxiang jiaxiang	(guu-shee-ahng); (jee-ah-shee- ahng)
homosexual	tongxinglian	(toong-sheeng- lee-in)
honey	fengmi mi	(fuung-me); (me)
Hong Kong	Xiang Guang	(Shee-ahng Gwahng)
hors d'oeuvres	lengpanr	(luung-pahn-urr)
horse	ma	(mah)
hospital	yiyuan	(ee-ywen)
host, owner	zhuren	(juu-wren)
hot	re	(ruh)
hotel	luguan	(luu-gwahn)
hot towel	re maojin	(ruh mou-jeen)
hot water	re shui	(ruh shway)
hour	xiaoshi	(shee-ow-shr)
house	fangwu	(fahng-wuu)
household	renjia	(wren-jee-ah)
housewife	funu	(fuu-nuu)
how	zenme	(zen-muh)

hungry	e	(uh)
hurry	henji	(hin-jee)
hurt, ache	teng	(tuung)
husband	zhangfu	(jahng-fuu)

I

ice	bing	(beeng)
ice cream	bing qilin	(beeng chee-leen)
ice hockey	bing qiu	(beeng cheo)
ice skating	hua bing	(hwah beeng)
ice skating rink	liu bing chang	(leo beeng chahng)
ice water	bing shui	(beeng shway)
ill, sick	youbing	(yoe-beeng)
illegal	buhefa-de	(buu-huh-fah-duh)
immediately	mashang	(mah-shahng)
immigrants	yimin	(ee-meen)
immigration	yimin jiancha zhan	(yee-meen jee-in-chah jahn)
Imperial Palace	Gu Gong	(Guu Goong)

import (item)	jinkou	(jeen-koe)
important	zhongyao	(joong-yow)
import duty	jinkou shui	(jeen-koe shway)
import license	jinkou xukezheng	(jeen-koe shu-kuh-jung)
impossible	bukeneng-de	(buu-kuh-nuung-duh)
income	shouru	(show-ruu)
income tax	suo-de shui	(swaw-duh shway)
incorrect	budui	(buu-dway)
indigestion	xiaohuabuliang	(shee-ow-hwah-buu-lee-ahng)
indoors	shinei	(shr-nay)
industry	gongye	(goong-yeh)
inexpensive	pianyi	(pee-in-ee)
infected	ganran	(gahn-rahn)
inflammation	fayan	(fah-yahn)
inflation	tonghuo pengzhang	(toong-hwaw puung-jahng)
informal	feizhenshi-de	(fay-jun-shr-duh)
information, news	xiaoxi	(shee-ow-she)
information desk	wenxunchu	(wun-shwun-chuu)
injection	zhushe	(juu-shuh)
injured	shoushang-le	(show-shahng-luh)

insect repellant	chuchongji	(chuu-choong-jee)
inside	li	(lee)
installment	fenqu ju kuan	(fun-chu juu kwahn)
insurance	baoxian	(bow-shee-in)
interest (money)	lixi	(lee-she)
interesting	youyisi	(yoe-ee-suh)
interest rate	lilu	(lee-luu)
intermission	mujian xiuxi	(muu-jee-in she-o-she)
international	guoji	(gwaw-jee)
international law	guoji fa	(gwaw-jee fah)
interpreter	fanyi	(fahn-ee)
intersection	shizilukour	(shr-dzu-luu-koe-urr)
into	jin	(jeen)
investment	touzi	(toe-dzu)
invitation	qingtie	(cheeng-tee-eh)
iron (clothing)	yun tang	(ywun); (tahng)
irrigation	guangai	(gwahn-guy)
is (in, on, at)	zai	(zigh)
island	dao	(dow)
it	ta	(tah)
item, article	wupin	(wuu-peen)
ivory	xiangya	(shee-ahng-yah)

J

jacket	duanshangyi	(dwahn-shahng-ee)
jade	yu	(yuu)
jail, prison	jianyu	(jee-in-yuu)
jam	guojiang	(gwaw-jee-ahng)
jazz	jueshiyinyue	(ju-eh-shr-een-yu-eh)
jeans	niuzaiku	(neo-zigh-kuu)
jeep	jipuche	(jee-puu-chuh)
jewelery	zhubao	(juu-bow)
job	gongzuo	(goong-zwaw)
jogging suit	yundongyi	(ywun-doong-ee)
joke (noun)	xiaohua	(shee-ow-hwah)
journalist	jizhe	(jee-juh)
journey	luxing	(luu-sheeng)
judge (noun)	faguan	(fah-gwahn)
judge (verb)	panduan	(pahn-dwahn)
judo	rou dao	(roe dow)
juice (fruit)	guozhi	(gwaw-jr)
jumper, sweater	maoyi	(mou-ee)
jungle	conglin	(tsoong-leen)
justice	gongzheng	(goong-juung)

karate	kongshoudao	(koong-show-dow)
kettle, pot	hu	(huu)
key	yaoshi	(yow-shr)
kilogram	gongjin	(goong-jeen)
kilometer	gongli	(goong-lee)
kind, type	zhong	(joong)
kindergarten	youeryuan	(yoe-urr-ywen)
kiss	wen	(wun)
kitchen	chufang	(chuu-fahng)
kite	fengzheng	(fuung-juung)
kleenex	zhijin	(jr-jeen)
knee	xigai	(she-guy)
knife	daozi	(dow-dzu)
know	zhidao	(jr-dow)
Kodak	Keda	(Kuh-dah)
Korea	Chaoxian	(Chow-shee-in)
Kyoto	Jingdu	(Jeeng-duu)

L

label (noun)	biaoqian	(bee-ow-chee-in)
labor	laodong	(lou-doong)
laboratory	shiyanshi	(shr-yahn-shr)
laborer	gongren	(goong-wren)
lacquerware	qiqi	(chee-chee)
lake	hu	(huu)
lamb (meat)	yangrou	(yahng-roe)
lamp	diandeng	(dee-in-duung)
land (earth)	tudi	(tuu-dee)
landlord	fangzhu	(fahng-juu)
landslide	fengjing	(fuung-jeeng)
lane	hutong	(huu-toong)
language	yuyan hua	(yuu-yahn); (hwah)
Lantern Festival	Deng Jie	(Duung Jee-eh)
late	wan	(wahn)
later	yihou	(ee-hoe)
large	dade	(dah-duh)
late	wan	(wahn)
Latin America	Lading Meizhou	(Lah-deeng May-joe)
laugh	xiao	(shee-ow)

laundry (clothing)	yaoxi-de yifu	(yow-she-duh ee-fuu);
(place)	xiyi dian	(she-ee dee-in)
laundry bag	xiyi dai	(she-ee die)
lavatory	cesuo	(tsuh-swaw)
law	falu	(fah-luu)
lawsuit	susong	(suu-soong)
lawyer	lushi	(luu-shr)
laxative	huanxieji	(hwahn-she-eh-jee)
lazy	landuo	(lahn-dwaw)
leader	lingdao	(leeng-dow)
learn	xuexi	(shu-eh-she)
leather	pige	(pee-guh)
leave (depart)	likai	(lee-kigh)
leave a message	liu hua	(leo hwah)
leave a note	liu tiao	(leo tee-ow)
lecture	jiangyan	(jee-ahng-yahn)
left side	zuobianr	(zwaw-bee-in-urr)
leg	tui	(tway)
legal	hefa	(huh-fah)
leisure time	kongxian shijian	(koong-shee-in shr-jee-in)
lemon	ningmeng	(neeng-muung)
lend	jie	(jee-eh)
lens (camera)	jingtou	(jeeng-toe)

lens cap	jingtougai	(jeeng-toe-guy)
letter	xin	(sheen)
letter of credit	xinyong zheng	(sheen-yoong juung)
letter paper	xin zhi	(sheen jr)
library	tushuguan	(tuu-shuu-gwahn)
license	xuke zheng	(shu-kuh juung)
lid	gai	(guy)
lift (elevator)	dianti	(dee-in-tee)
light (weight)	qingde	(cheeng-duh)
lightning	shandian	(shahn-dee-in)
like	xihuan	(she-hwahn)
lipstick	kouhong	(koe-hoong)
liquor	baijiu	(buy-jeo)
liter	sheng	(shuung)
literature	wenxue	(wun-shu-eh)
little	shao	(shou)
live	zhu	(juu)
liver	gan	(gahn)
living room	keting	(kuh-teeng)
lobster	longxia	(loong-shee-ah)
lock	suo	(swaw)
long	chang	(chahng)
long-distance	changtu	(chahng-tuu)
longevity	changshou	(chahng-show)

Los Angeles	Luo Shanji	(Lwaw Shahn-jee)
lose	diushi	(deo-shr)
lost and found	shiwu zhaoling	(shr-wuu jow-leeng)
loud	chao	(chow)
lounge	xiuxishi	(sheo-she-shr)
love (verb)	ai	(eye)
luck	yunqi	(ywun-chee)
luggage	xingli	(sheeng-lee)
luggage rack	xinglijia	(sheeng-lee-jee-ah)
lunar calendar	yin li nong li	(een lee); (noong lee)
lunch	zhongfan	(joong-fahn)
lung	fei	(fay)
lychees	lizhi	(lee-jr)

M

Macao	Aomen	(Ow-mun)
machine	jiqi	(jee-chee)
magazine	zazhi	(zah-jr)
magic	moshu	(mwo-shuu)

magician	moshushi	(mwo-shuu-shr)
mahjong	majiang	(mah-jee-ahng)
mail (noun)	youjian	(yoe-jee-in)
mail (verb)	ji	(jee)
mainland	dalu	(dah-luu)
main station	zong zhan	(zoong jahn)
maitre d'	zongguan	(zoong-gwahn)
make	zuo	(zwaw)
makeup	huazhuang	(hwah-jwahng)
male	nan	(nahn)
man, male	nanren	(nahn-wren)
management	guanli	(gwahn-lee)
manager	jingli	(jeeng-lee)
mango	mangguo	(mahng-gwaw)
man-made	ren-zao	(wren-zow)
manufacture	shengchan	(shuung-chahn)
many	duo	(dwaw)
map	ditu	(dee-tuu)
market	shichang	(shr-chahng)
market price	shichang jiage	(shr-chahng jee-ah-guh)
marketing	shichang yingxiao	(shr-chahng eeng-shee-ow)
married	yijing jiehun-de	(ee-jeeng jee-eh-hwun-duh)
marry (verb)	jiehun	(jee-eh-hwun)

martial arts	wu shu	(wuu shuu)
mask (for mouth)	kouzhao	(koe-jow)
massage	anmo	(ahn-mwo)
match, race	sai	(sigh)
matches	huochai	(hwaw-chigh)
mattress	chuangdian	(chwahng-dee-in)
me	wo	(waw)
meal	fan	(fahn)
measure (verb)	celiang	(tsuh-lee-ahng)
meat	rou	(roe)
mechanic	jigong	(jee-goong)
medicine	yiyao	(ee-yow)
meet	huijian	(hway-jee-in)
meeting	hui	(hway)
melon	gua	(gwaw)
memorial hall	jinian guan	(jee-nee-in gwahn)
menu	caidan	(tsigh-dahn)
message	liuhua	(leo-hwah)
metal	jinshu	(jeen-shuu)
meter	gongchi	(goong-chee)
metric ton	gong dun	(goong dwun)
microphone	huatong	(hwah-toong)
middle	zhongjian	(joong-jee-in)
midnight	wuye	(wuu-yuh)
military	junshi	(jwin-shr)

milk	niunai	(neo-nigh)
milliliter	haosheng	(how-shuung)
millimeter	haomi	(how-me)
million	baiwan	(buy-wahn)
mineral water	kuangquan shui	(kwahng-chwahn shway)
miniskirt	chao duanqun	(chow dwahn-chwun)
minority (people)	shaoshu minzu	(shou-shuu meen-zuu)
minute	fen	(fin)
mirror	jingzi	(jeeng-dzu)
miscellaneous goods	za huo	(zah hwaw)
mistake	cuowu	(tswaw-wuu)
Mitsubishi	Sanling	(Sahn-leeng)
mixed	za	(zah)
model (person)	moter	(mwo-tuh-urr)
monastery	siyuan	(suh-ywen)
money	qian	(chee-in)
money order	hui piao	(hway pee-ow)
monk	heshang	(huh-shahng)
monkey	houzi	(hoe-dzu)
monosodium glutamate	weijing	(way-jeeng)
monument	jinianbei	(jee-nee-in-bay)
moon	yueliang	(yu-eh-lee-ahng)

morals, morality	dao-de	(dow-duh)
morning	zaoshang	(zow-shahng)
Moscow	Mosike	(Mwo-suh-kuh)
Moslem	Qingzhen	(Cheeng-jun)
mosquito	wenzi	(wun-dzu)
mother	muqin	(muu-cheen)
motorbike	motuoche	(mwo-twaw-chuh)
mountain	shan	(shahn)
mountain peak	shan feng	(shahn fuung)
mouth	kou	(koe);
	zui	(zway)
movie	dianying	(dee-in-eeng);
(television)	dianshiju	(dee-in-shr-juu)
movie theater	dianying yuan	(dee-in-eeng ywen)
muscles	jirou	(jee-roe)
museum	bowuguan	(bwo-wuu-gwahn)
mushroom	mogu	(mwo-guu)
music	yinyue	(een-yu-eh)
musical instrument	yueqi	(yu-eh-chee)
Muslim	Qingzhen	(Cheeng-jun)
mustard	jiemo	(jee-eh-mwo)
mutton	yangrou	(yahng-roe)
my, mine	wo-de	(waw-duh)
myself	woziji	(waw-dzu-jee)

nail (finger)	zhijia	(jr-jee-ah)
nail clippers	zhijiadao	(jr-jee-ah-dow)
name	xingming	(sheeng-meeng)
nanny (for baby)	baomu	(bow-muu)
nap	xiaoshui	(shee-ow-shway)
napkin	canjin	(tsahn-jeen)
narrow, cramped	xiazhai	(shee-ah-jigh)
nation	guo	(gwaw)
national (adjective)	guojia	(gwaw-jee-ah)
national anthem	guoge	(gwaw-guh)
national defense	guofang	(gwaw-fahng)
national flag	guoqi	(gwaw-chee)
nationality	minzu	(meen-zuu)
native dress	guofu	(gwaw-fuu)
native place	kuxiang	(kuu-shee-ahng)
navy	haijun	(high-jwin)
near	jin	(jeen)
neck	bozi	(bwo-dzu)
necklace	xianglian	(shee-ahng-lee-in)
necktie	lingdai	(leeng-die)
need	xuyao	(shu-yow)

needle	zhen	(jun)
negative (film)	dipian	(dee-pee-in)
neighbor	linju	(leen-juu)
Netherlands	Helan	(Huh-lahn)
new	xin	(sheen)
news	xinwen	(sheen-wun)
newspaper	baozhi	(bow-jr)
New Year	Xin Nian Yuandan	(Sheen Nee-in); (Ywen-dahn)
New Year's Eve	Chu Xi	(Chuu She)
New York	Niu Yue	(Neo Yu-eh)
next	xia	(shee-ah)
next to	pangbianr	(pahng-bee-in-urr)
night	ye	(yeh)
nightclub	ye zonghui	(yeh joong-hway)
nightlife	ye shenghuo	(yeh shuung-hwaw)
noisy	chao	(chow)
noodles	miantiao	(mee-in-tee-ow)
noodle shop	mian guanr	(mee-in gwahn-rr)
noon	zhongwu	(joong-wuu)
normal	zhengcheng	(juung-chuung)
north	bei	(bay)
North America	Bei Meizhou	(Bay May-joe)

Northeast China	Dong Bei	(Doong Bay)
northern	beifang	(bay-fahng)
nose	bizi	(bee-dzu)
notebook	bijiben	(bee-jee-bin)
not enough	bu gou	(buu go)
not good	bu hao	(buu how)
no trespassing	jinzhi tongxing	(jeen-jr toong-sheeng)
novel	xiaoshuo	(shee-ow-shwaw)
novelist	xiaoshuojia	(shee-ow-shwaw-jee-ah)
nuclear	he	(huh)
number	haoma	(how-mah)
nurse	hushi	(huu-shr)
nursery	tuoersuo	(twaw-urr-swaw)
nutrition	yingyang	(eeng-yahng)

O

oatmeal	maipian	(my-pee-in)
occupation	zhiye	(jr-yeh)
occupied	youren	(yoe-wren)
ocean	haiyang	(high-yahng)

office	bangongshi	(bahn-goong-shr)
office hours	bangong shijian	(bahn-goong shr-jee-in);
	yingye shijian	(eeng-yeh shr-jee-in)
office worker	zhi yuan	(jr ywen)
official	guan	(gwahn)
official business	gong wu	(goong wuu)
often	changchang	(chahng-chahng)
oil	you	(yoe)
oil field	you tian	(yoe tee-in)
ointment	yaogao	(yow-gow)
old (person)	lao	(lou)
old man (people)	lao ren	(lou wren)
old thing	jiu	(jew)
old woman	lao taitai	(lou tie-tie)
on, on top of	shang	(shahng)
once	yici	(ee-tsu)
one	yi-ge	(ee-guh)
one-child policy	dusheng zinu zhengce	(duu-shuung dzu-nuu jung-tsuh)
one-way	dan-cheng	(dahn-chuung)
one-way ticket	dancheng piao	(dahn-chuung pee-ow)
only	zhi	(jr)
open (shop)	kaimen	(kigh-mun)

open (sign)	yingyezhong	(eeng-yeh-joong)
open-date ticket	bu dingqi piao	(buu deeng-chee pee-ow)
opera	geju	(guh-juu)
(Beijing opera)	jingju	(jeeng-juu)
opium	yapian	(yah-pee-in)
opportunity	jihui	(jee-hway)
orange (fruit)	ganzi	(gahn-dzu)
orange juice	juzi zhi	(juu-dzu jr)
order	jiao	(jee-ow)
ordinary	putong-de	(puu-toong-duh)
ordinary train	putong che	(puu-toong chuh)
organization	zuzhi	(zuu-jr)
oriental	dongfang	(doong-fahng)
out	chu	(chuu)
outlet (electric)	chazuo	(chah-zwaw)
out of order	huaile	(hwie-luh)
outside	waibian	(wigh-bee-in)
outside line	wai xian	(wigh shee-in)
over	shangbianr	(shahng-bee-in-urr)
overcoat	dayi	(dah-ee)
overnight	yiye	(ee-yeh)
overseas	guowai	(gwaw-wigh)
Overseas Chinese	Hua Qiao	(Hwah Chee-ow)
overseas edition	haiwai ban	(high-wigh bahn)

overview	zongdekanfa	(zoong-duh-kahn-fah)
owe	qian	(chee-in)
owner	suoyouren	(swaw-yoe-wren)
ox	gongniu	(goong-neo)
oxygen	yangqi	(yahng-chee)
oyster	hao	(how)

P

Pacific Ocean	Taiping Yang	(Tie-peeng Yahng)
pack (suitcase)	da xingli	(dah sheeng-lee)
package	baoguo	(bow-gwaw)
paddy field	dao tian	(dow tee-in)
padlock	guasuo	(gwah-swaw)
pagoda	baota	(bow-tah)
painful	henteng	(hin-tuung)
paint, draw	hua	(hwah)
painting	huar	(hwah-urr)
pair, couple	dui	(dway)
pajamas	shuiyi	(shway-ee)
palace	gongdian	(goong-dee-in)

panda bear	xiongmao	(shee-ong-mou)
pants, slacks	kuzi	(kuu-dzu)
pantyhose	liankuwa	(lee-in-kuu-wah)
paper	zhi	(jr)
paper currency	zhibi	(jr-bee)
paradise	tiantang	(tee-in-tahng)
parcel	baoguo	(bow-gwaw)
parents	fumu	(fuu-muu)
Paris	Bali	(Bah-lee)
park (car) (public)	ting che gongyuan	(teeng chuh); (goong-ywen)
parking lot	tingche chang	(teeng-chuh chahng)
partial payment	bufen fukuan	(buu-fin fuu-kwahn)
partner	huoban	(hwaw-bahn)
party (gathering)	juhui	(juu-hway)
party (political)	dang	(dahng)
party member	dang yuan	(dahng ywen)
passenger	luke	(luu-kuh)
passport	huzhao	(huu-jow)
passport number	huzhao haoma	(huu-jow how-mah)
pastry	gaodian	(gow-dee-in)
pastry shop	gaodian dian	(gow-dee-in dee-in)
patent	zhuanli	(jwahn-lee)

path	xiaolu	(shee-ow-luu)
patience	naixin	(nigh-sheen)
patient	bingren	(beeng-wren)
pavilion	tingzi	(teeng-dzu)
pay (verb)	fuqian	(fuu-chee-in)
payment	fukuan	(fuu-kwahn)
peace	heping	(huh-peeng)
peaches	taozi	(tou-dzu)
peak, summit	shanding	(shahn-deeng)
peanuts	huasheng	(hwah-shuung)
Pearl River	Zhu Jiang	(Juu Jee-ahng)
pearls	zhenzhu	(jun-juu)
pears	li	(lee)
peasant	nongmin	(noong-meen)
pedestrian	xingren	(sheeng-wren)
pedicab	sanlunche	(sahn-lwun-chuh)
Peking duck	Beijing kaoya	(Bay-jeeng kow-yah)
pen	bi	(bee)
pencil	qianbi	(chee-in-bee)
penicillin	qingmeisu	(cheeng-may-suu)
penknife	xiaodao	(shee-ow-dow)
people	ren	(wren)
pepper	hujiao	(huu-jee-ow)

perfect	wanmei	(wahn-may)
performance	yanchu	(yahn-chuu)
performer	yanyuan	(yahn-ywen)
perfume	xiangshui	(shee-ahng-shway)
periodical	qikan	(chee-kahn)
permission	xuke	(shu-kuh)
permit (noun)	zukezheng	(zuu-kuh-juung)
permit, allow	yunxu	(ywun-shu)
person	ren	(wren)
personal	sirende	(suh-wren-duh)
personality	gexing	(guh-sheeng)
perspire	chuhan	(chuu-hahn)
petroleum	shiyou	(shr-yoe)
pharmacy	yaodian	(yow-dee-in)
Philadelphia	Feicheng	(Fay-chuung)
phone call (long-distance)	dian hua changtu dian hua	(dee-in hwah); (chahng-tuu dee-in hwah)
photocopy	fuyin	(fuu-een)
photograph	zhaopian	(jow pee-in)
physical exam	ti jian	(tee jee-in)
physical exercise	tiyu	(tee-yuu)
picnic	yecan huican	(yeh-tsahn); (hway-tsahn)
picnic basket	yecan shilan	(yeh-tsahn shr-lahn)

picture	huar	(hwah-urr)
piece, lump	kuai	(kwie)
pig	zhu	(juu)
pill	pian	(pee-in)
pillow	zhentou	(jun-toe)
pillowcase	zhentao	(jun-tou)
pineapple	boluo	(bwo-lwaw)
ping-pong	pingpangqiu	(peeng-pahng-cheo)
place	difang	(dee-fahng)
plain, flatland	pingyuan	(peeng-ywen)
plane	feiji	(fay-jee)
plants	zhiwu	(jr-wuu)
plate	panzi	(pahn-dzu)
platform (train)	zhantai	(jahn-tie)
play (verb)	wanr youxi	(wahn-urr); (yoe-she)
play (theater)	xiju	(she-juu)
player, athlete	yundongyuan	(ywun-doong-ywen)
playground	caochang	(tsow-chahng)
please	qing	(cheeng)
plug (electric)	chatou	(chah-toe)
plum	lizi	(lee-dzu)
poached egg	shuipudan	(shway-puu-dahn)
poems, songs	shige	(shr-guh)

poet	shiren	(shr-wren)
poison	duwu	(duu-wuu)
police	jingcha	(jeeng-chah)
police station	gongganju	(goong-gahn-juu)
politics	zhengzhi	(juung-jr)
pollution	wuran	(wuu-rahn)
pond	chitang	(chee-tahng)
pool	chi	(chee)
poor	youyongchi	(yoe-yoong-chee)
population	renkou	(wren-koe)
porcelain	ciqi	(tsu-chee)
pork	zhurou	(juu-roe)
port	matou	(mah-toe)
postage	youfei	(yoe-fay)
postage stamp	youpiao	(yoe-pee-ow)
postcard	mingxin pian	(meeng-sheen pee-in)
post office	youju	(yoe-juu)
potato	tudou	(tuu-doe)
pottery	taoqi	(tou-chee)
pound	bang	(bahng)
prawn	xia	(shee-ah)
pregnant	huaiyun	(hwie-ywun)
premier	zongli	(zoong-lee)
prepare	zhubei	(juu-bay)
prescription	yaofang	(yow-fahng)

present (gift)	liwu	(lee-wuu)
president		
(corporate)	zongcai	(zoong-tsigh)
(national)	zongtong	(zoong-toong)
pretty	piaoliang	(pee-ow-lee-ahng)
price	jiaqian	(jee-ah-chee-in);
	jiage	(jee-ah-guh)
priest	jiaoshi	(jee-ow-shr)
primary school	xiao xue	(shee-ow shu-eh)
printed matter	yinshua pin	(een-shwah peen)
printing plant	yinshua chang	(een-shwah chahng)
prison	jianyu	(jee-in-yuu)
private	siren	(suh-wren)
problem	wenti	(wun-tee)
process (film)	chongxi	(choong-she)
product	chanpin	(chahn-peen)
profession	zhiye	(jr-yeh)
professional	zhuanye-de	(jwahn-yeh-duh)
profit	lirun	(lee-rwun)
program	jiemu	(jee-eh-muu)
promise	daying	(dah-eeng)
pronunciation	fayin	(fah-een)
property	caichan	(tsigh-chahn)
prostitute	jinu	(jee-nuu)

Protestant	Xinjiao	(Sheen-jee-ow)
province	sheng	(shuung)
prune	meizi	(may-dzu)
psychology	xinlixue	(sheen-lee-shu-eh)
public	gonggong	(goong-goong)
public relations	gonggong guanxi	(goong-goong gwahn-she)
Public Security Bureau	Gong Anju	(Goong Ahn-juu)
public square	guang chang	(gwahng chahng)
publish	chuban	(chuu-bahn)
pupil	xuesheng	(shu-eh-shuung)
purchasing agent	daigou ren	(die-go wren)
pure	chunde	(chwun-duh)
purse, handbag	shoutibao	(show-tee-bow)

Q

quality	zhiliang	(jr-lee-ahng)
quantity	shuliang	(shuu-lee-ahng)
question, problem	wenti	(wun-tee)

queue	paidui	(pie-dway)
quick, fast	kuai	(kwie)
quiet, peaceful	anjing	(ahn-jeeng)
quilt	beizi	(bay-dzu)
quiz, test	kaoshi	(kow-shr)
quota	ding-e	(deeng-uh)

R

race	zhongzupian	(joong-zuu-pee-in)
racism	zhongzupianjian	(joong-zuu-pee-in-jee-in)
radio	shouyinji	(show-een-jee)
railway	tielu	(tee-eh-luu)
railway station	huochezhan	(hwaw-chuh-jahn)
rain (noun)	yushui	(yuu-shway)
rain (verb)	xiayu	(shee-ah-yuu)
rainbow	caihong	(tsigh-hoong)
raincoat	yuyi	(yuu-ee)
rainstorm	baofengyu	(bow-fuung-yuu)
rape	qiangjian	(chee-ahng-jee-in)

rash	zhenzi	(jun-dzu)
rat	haozi	(how-dzu)
rate, price	jiage	(jee-ah-guh)
raw	sheng-de	(shuung-duh)
razor	tidao	(tee-dow)
razor blades	tidao pian	(tee-dow pee-in)
read	kan	(kahn)
read a book	kan shu	(kahn shuu)
reading room	yuelan shi	(yu-eh-lahn shr)
ready	hao-le	(how-luh)
real	zhen-de	(jun-duh)
realtor	dichan jingji ren	(dee-chahn jeeng-jee wren)
receipt	shouju	(show-juu)
reception, party	zhaodaihui	(jow-die-hway)
reception desk	fuwutai	(fuu-wuu-tie)
receptionist	jiedaiyuan	(jee-eh-die-ywen)
recommend	tuijian	(tway-jee-in)
record	changpian	(chahng-pee-in)
recreation, games	yule	(yuu-luh)
refresh oneself	jiefa	(jee-eh-fah)
refrigerator	bingxiang	(beeng-shee-ahng)
refugee	binanzhe	(bee-nahn-juh)
refund	tuikuan tuiqian	(tway-kwahn); (tway-chee-in)

region	diqu	(dee-chu)
registered (mail)	guahao	(gwah-how)
regulation	guilu	(gway-luh)
relationship	guanxi	(gwahn-she)
relative, kin	qinqi	(cheen-chee)
religion	zongjiao	(zoong-jee-ow)
rent, hire	zu	(zuu)
rent (money)	zujin	(zuu-jeen)
repair	xiu	(sheo)
repeat	zai shuo	(zigh shwaw)
report (official)	baogao	(bow-gow)
representative	daibiao	(die-bee-ow)
reservation	yuding	(yuu-deeng)
reservation desk	yuding chu	(yuu-deeng chuu)
reserve	ding	(deeng)
residence permit	juliu zheng	(juu-leo jung)
residential area	zhuzhaiqu	(juu-jigh-chu)
responsibility	zeren	(zuh-wren)
rest	xiuxi	(sheo-she)
restaurant	fanguan	(fahn-gwahn)
return, come back	huiqu	(hway-chu)
return, give back	huan	(hwahn)
return ticket	laihui piao	(lie-hway pee-ow)

reverse charges	duifangfufei	(dway-fahng-fuu-fay)
revolution	geming	(guh-meeng)
rice (cooked)	baifan	(buy-fahn)
rice (uncooked)	mi	(me)
rich	fuyou	(fuu-yoe)
ride (bike or horse)	qi	(chee)
ride in, go by	zuo	(zwaw)
right	you	(yoe)
right side	youbianr	(yoe-bee-in-urr)
ring (jewelry)	jiezhi	(jee-eh-jr)
ripe	chengshou	(chuung-show)
river	he	(huh)
road	lu	(luu)
roast; roasted	kao shao	(kow); (shou)
rob, steal	daoqie	(dow-chee-eh)
rock	yanshi	(yahn-shr)
romanization	luomahua	(lwaw-mah-hwah)
roof	wuding	(wuu-deeng)
room	fangjian	(fahng-jee-in)
room number	fangjian haoma	(fahng-jee-in how-mah)
rotten	fulan-de	(fuu-lahn-duh)
round-trip	laihui	(lie-hway)

round-trip ticket	laihui piao	(lie-hway pee-ow)
route	lu	(luu)
row, line, queue	pai	(pie)
rubbish	laji	(lah-jee)
rug (small)	xiao ditan	(shee-ow dee-tahn)
ruins	jiuzhi	(jeo-jr)
run	paobu	(pow-buu)

S

sack, bag	koudai	(koe-die)
safe (adjective)	anquan	(ahn-chwahn)
safe (noun)	baoxianxiang	(bow-shee-in-shee-ahng)
salad	sala	(sah-lah)
salary	xinshui	(sheen-shway)
sale	xiaoshou	(shee-ow-show)
sales manager	xiaoshou jingli	(shee-ow-show jeeng-lee)
salesperson	dianyuan	(dee-in-ywen)
sales tax	yingye shui	(eeng-yeh shway)
salt	yan	(yahn)

salt water	yan shui	(yahn shway)
same	yiyang	(ee-yahng)
sample	yangping biaoben	(yahng-peeng); (bee-ow-bin)
sandals	liangxie	(lee-ahng-she-eh)
sandwich	sanmingzhi	(sahn-meeng-jr)
San Francisco	Jiujin Shan	(Jew-jeen Shahn)
sanitary towel	weishengjing	(way-shuung-jeeng)
satellite	weixing	(way-sheeng)
sausage	xiangchang	(shee-ahng-chahng)
save money	shengqian	(shuung-chee-in)
save, rescue	qiangjiu	(chee-ahng-jeo)
savor, taste	wei	(way)
scarf	weijin	(way-jeen)
scenery	fengjing jingse	(fuung-jeeng); (jeeng-suh)
schedule	richengbiao	(rr-chuung-bee-ow)
scholar	xuezhe	(shu-eh-juh)
school	xuexiao	(shu-eh-shee-ow)
schoolmate	tongxue	(toong-shu-eh)
scientist	kexuejia	(kuh-shu-eh-jee-ah)
scissors	jiandao	(jee-ahn-dow)
scrambled eggs	chao jidan	(chow jee-dahn)

screwdriver	gaizhui	(guy-jway)
sculpture	diaoxiang	(dow-shee-ahng)
sea	hai	(high)
seafood	haixian yuxia lei	(high-shee-in); (yuu-shee-ah lay)
seal, stamp	tuzhang	(tuu-jahng)
seashore, beach	haitan haibin	(high-tahn) (high-bin)
seasick	yunchuan-de	(ywun-chwahn- duh)
season	jijie	(jee-jee-eh)
seat	zuowei	(zwaw-way)
seatbelt	anquan dai	(ahn-chwahn die)
second class	er deng	(urr duung)
second time	miao	(mee-ow)
secret	mimi	(me-me)
secretary	mishu	(me-shuu)
section in office	ke	(kuh)
section, part	bufen	(buu-fin)
security guard	anquan renyuan	(ahn-chwahn wren-ywen)
see	jian kanjian	(jee-in); (kahn-jee-in)
See you again.	Zai jian.	(Zigh jee-in.)
sell	shoumai	(show-my)
selling price	mai jia	(my jee-ah)

seminar	yantaohui	(yahn-tou-hway)
send (post)	ji	(jee)
send back	songhui	(soong-hway)
send C.O.D.	huodao fukuan	(hwaw-dow fuu-kwahn)
sentence in court	panxing	(pahn-sheeng)
Seoul	Hancheng	(Hahn-chuung)
separate	fenkai-de	(fin-kigh-duh)
serious	yansu	(yahn-suu)
serious (injury)	yanzhong-de	(yahn-joong-duh)
service	fuwu	(fuu-wuu)
service attendant	fuwu yuan	(fuu-wuu ywen)
service desk	fuwu tai	(fuu-wuu tie)
service fee	fuwu fei	(fuu-wuu fay)
several	xie	(she-eh)
sew	feng	(fuung)
sex	xing	(sheeng)
shake hands	wo shou	(waw show)
shampoo	xifaji	(she-fah-jee)
shave	gualian guahuzi	(gwah-lee-in); (gwah-huu-dzu)
she	ta	(tah)
shed, shack	pengzi	(puung-dzu)
sheep	yang	(yahng)
sheet	beidan	(bay-dahn)
ship	haichuan	(high-chwahn)

shipment	zhuangyun	(jwahng-ywun)
shirt	chenshan	(chun-shahn)
shoelaces	xie dai	(she-eh die)
shoe polish	xie you	(she-eh yoe)
shoes	xie	(she-eh)
shop	shangdian	(shahng-dee-in)
shopping area	shangyequ	(shahng-yeh-chu)
shore	an	(ahn)
short	duan	(dwahn)
short (height)	ai	(eye)
shorts	duanku	(dwahn-kuu)
show, movie	fangying	(fahng-eeng)
show, performance	biaoyan	(bee-ow-yahn)
shower	linyu	(leen-yuu)
shrimp	xia	(shee-ah)
shut	guan	(gwahn)
shy	haixiu	(high-shee-ow)
Siberia	Xiboliya	(She-bwo-lee-yah)
sick	shengbing	(shuung-beeng)
sidewalk	renxingdao	(wren-sheeng-dow)
sightseeing	youlan	(yoe-lahn)
sign	biaoyupai	(bee-ow-yuu-pie)
signature	qianming	(chee-in-meeng)

silk	sichou	(suh-choe)
silk factory	sichou chang	(suh-choe chahng)
Silk Road	Sichou Zhi Lu	(Suh-choe Jr Luu)
silver	yin	(een)
simple	jiandan	(jee-in-dahn)
sing	changge	(chahng-guh)
single, unmarried	danshen	(dahn-shuun)
single room	danjian	(dahn-jee-in)
single ticket	danchengpiao	(dahn-chuung-pee-ow)
sister (older)	jiejie	(jee-eh-jee-eh)
(younger)	meimie	(may-me-eh)
sit	zuo	(zwaw)
sitting room	tangwu	(tahng-wuu)
size	daxiao	(dah-shee-ow)
size (clothes)	chicun	(chee-tswun)
skating	liubing	(leo-beeng)
skating rink	liubing chang	(leo-beeng chahng)
ski (snow)	hua xue	(hwah shu-eh)
(water)	hua shui	(hwah shway)
skin	pifu	(pee-fuu)
skirt	qunzi	(chwun-dzu)
sky	tiankong	(tee-in-koong)
sleep, go to sleep	shuijiao	(shway-jee-ow)

sleeping berth	wo pu	(waw puu)
sleeping car	wo che	(waw chuh)
sleepy	kun	(kwun)
slipper	tuoxie	(twaw-she-eh)
slogan	biaoyu	(bee-ow-yuu)
slope	po	(pwaw)
slow	man	(mahn)
small	xiao	(shee-ow)
small change	lingqian	(leeng-chee-in)
smelly	chou	(choe)
smile	xiao	(shee-ow)
snack	xiaochi	(shee-ow-chee)
snake	she	(shuh)
snow (noun)	xue	(shu-eh)
snow (verb)	xiaxue	(shee-ah-shu-eh)
snowplow	saoxue ji	(sow-shu-eh jee)
soap	feizao	(fay-zow)
soccer	zuqiu	(zuu-cheo)
socialism	shehuizhuyi	(shuh-hway-juu-ee)
society	shehui	(shuh-hway)
socket (electric)	chazuo	(chah-zwaw)
socks, stockings	wazi	(wah-dzu)
soda water	qi shui	(chee shway)
sofa	shafa	(shah-fah)
soft	rouruan	(roe-rwahn)

soft drink	qingliang yinliao	(cheeng-lee-ahng een-lee-ow)
soldier	zhanshi	(jahn-shr)
some	yixie	(ee-she-eh)
son	erzi	(urr-dzu)
son-in-law	nuxu	(nuu-shu)
song	ge	(guh)
song lyrics	ge ci	(guh tsu)
sound	shengyin	(shuung-een)
soup	tang	(tahng)
sour taste	suan	(swahn)
south	nan	(nahn)
South China Sea	Nan Hai	(Nahn High)
southern part	nan fang	(nahn fahng)
souvenir	jinianpin	(jee-nee-in-peen)
souvenir shop	jinianpin dian	(jee-nee-in-peen dee-in)
soybean	huang dou	(hwahng doe)
soy sauce	jiang you	(jee-ahng yoe)
space shuttle	hangtian feiji	(hahng-tee-in fay-jee)
Spain	Xibanya	(She-bahn-yah)
spare time	ye yu	(yeh yuu)
speak	shuo shuohua	(shwaw); (shwaw-hwah)
special	tebie	(tuh-bee-eh)
spicy	la	(lah)

spoon	shaozi	(shou-dzu)
sporting goods	tiyu yongpin	(tee-yuu yoong-peen)
sports	yudong	(yuu-doong)
sports field	caochang	(tsow-chahng)
sprain	niushang	(neo-shahng)
spring	chuntian	(chwun-tee-in)
Spring Festival	Chun Jie	(Chwun Jee-eh)
square (place)	guangchang	(gwahng-chahng)
squid	youyu	(yoe-yuu)
stadium	tiyuchang	(tee-yuu-chahng)
stairs	louti	(low-tee)
stale	buxinxian	(buu-sheen-shee-in)
stamp	youpiao	(yoe-pee-ow)
stand in line	paidui	(pie-dway)
star	xingxing	(sheeng-sheeng)
start	kaishi	(kigh-shr)
station	zhan	(jahn)
stationery	wenju	(wun-juu)
stationery store	wenju dian	(wun-juu dee-in)
statue	diaoxiang	(dee-ow-shee-ahng)
stay	tingliu	(teeng-leo)
steal	tou	(toe)
steamed	zheng	(juung)

steamed bun	mantou	(mahn-toe)
steel	gang	(gahng)
stir-fried	chao	(chow)
stomach	wei	(way)
stop (verb)	ting	(teeng)
Stop!	Zhanzhu!	(Jahn-juu!)
stop a vehicle	che zhan	(chuh jahn)
store (shop)	shangdian	(shahng-dee-in)
storm	fengbao	(fuung-bow)
story, narrative	gushi	(guu-shr)
stove	huolu luzi	(hwaw-luu); (luu-dzu)
straight ahead	yizhi	(ee-jr)
stranger	moshengren	(mwo-shuung-wren)
strawberries	caomei	(tsow-may)
street	jie	(jee-eh)
strong	youli	(yoe-lee)
student	xuesheng	(shu-eh-shuung)
study	shufang	(shuu-fahng)
study abroad	liuxue	(leo-shu-eh)
style, appearance	yangshi	(yahng-shr)
suburbs	jiaoqu	(jee-ow-chu)
subway	ditie	(dee-tee-eh)
subway station	ditie chezhan	(dee-tee-eh chuh-jahn)

success	chenggong	(chuung-goong)
sugar	tang	(tahng)
suit (western)	xifu	(she-fuu)
suitcase	xiangzi	(shee-ahng-dzu)
suite	yitao fangjian	(ee-tou fahng-jee-in)
summer	xiatian	(shee-ah-tee-in)
Summer Palace	Yihe Yuan	(Yee-huh Ywen)
sun	taiyang	(tie-yahng)
sunburn	shaishang	(shy-shahng)
Sunday	Xingqitian	(Sheeng-chee-tee-in)
sunglasses	majing	(mah-jeeng)
sunshine	yangguang	(yahng-gwahng)
suntan lotion	shaiheigao	(shy-hay-gow)
Sun Yatsen	Sun Zhongshan	(Suun Joong-shahn)
supermarket	chaojishichang	(chow-jee-shr-chahng)
surface mail	putong youjian	(puu-toong yoe-jee-in)
sweat	han	(hahn)
sweater	maoyi	(mou-ee)
sweet	tian	(tee-in)
swim	youyong	(yoe-yoong)
swimming pool	youyong chi	(yoe-yoong chee)
swimsuit	youyong yi	(yoe-yoong ee)

315

switch (electric)	kaiguan	(kigh-gwahn)
switchboard	zongji	(zoong-jee)
switch off	guandiao	(gwahn-dee-ow)
switch on	dakai	(dah-kigh)
swollen	zhongle	(joong-luh)
sword	jian	(jee-in)
symphony	jiaoxiangyue	(jee-ow-shee-ahng-yu-eh)
symptoms (illness)	zhengzhuang	(juung-jwahng)
system	xitong	(she-toong)

T

table	zhuozi	(jwaw-dzu)
tablecloth	zhuo bu	(jwaw buu)
table lamp	taideng	(tie-duung)
table tennis	pingpangqiu	(peeng-pahng-cheo)
tailor	caifeng	(tsigh-fuung)
talks, meeting	huitan	(hway-tahn)
tangerine	juzi	(juu-dzu)
Taoism	Daizou Daojiao	(Die-zoe); (Dow-jee-ow)

tape recorder	cidai luyinji	(tsu-die luu-een-jee)
tariff	guanshui	(gwahn-shway)
taste, flavor	wei	(way)
tasty	haochi	(how-chee)
tax	shui	(shway)
tax free	mian shui	(mee-in shway)
taxi	chuzuqiche	(chuu-zuu-chee-chuh)
tea	cha	(chah)
teach	jiao	(jee-ow)
teacher	jiaoshi	(jee-ow-shr)
teacup	cha bei	(chah bay)
teahouse	cha guan	(chah gwahn)
team	dui	(dway)
teapot	cha hu	(chah huu)
teaspoon	tang chi	(tahng chee)
technical transfer	jishu zhuanrang	(jee-shuu jwahn-rahng)
technology	jishu gongyi	(jee-shuu); (goong-ee)
telephone (public phone)	dianhua gongyong dianhua	(dee-in-hwah); (goong-yoong dee-in hwah)
telephone booth	dianhua ting	(dee-in-hwah teeng)
telephone directory	dianhua bu	(dee-in-hwah buu)

telephone long-distance	changtu dianhua	(chahng-tuu dee-in-hwah)
telephone set	dianhua ji	(dee-in-hwah jee)
telephoto lens	wangyuan jingtou	(wahng-ywen jeeng-toe)
television	dianshi	(dee-in-shr)
tell	gaosu	(gow-suu)
temperature (body) (weather) (centigrade) (Fahrenheit)	wendu tiwen qiwen sheshi huashi	(wun-duu); (tee-wun); (chee-wun); (shuh-shr); (hwah-shr)
temple	siyuan	(suh-ywen)
tennis	wangqiu	(wahng-cheo)
tennis court	wangqiu chang	(wahng-cheo chahng)
tennis match	wangqiu sai	(wahng-cheo sigh)
test	kaoshi	(kow-shr)
tetanus	poshangfeng	(pwaw-shahng-fuung)
Thailand	Taiguo	(Tie-gwaw)
thank you	xiexie	(she-eh-she-eh)
that	na	(nah)
theater	juchang	(juu-chahng)
theater ticket	xipiao	(she-pee-ow)
them	tamen	(tah-mun)

there	nar	(nah-urr)
there is, are	you	(yoe)
thermometer	wendubiao	(wun-duu-bee-ow)
thermos bottle	nuanshuiping	(nwahn-shway-peeng)
these	zhe	(juh);
	zhei	(jay)
they	tamen	(tah-mun)
thick	hou	(hoe)
thief	zei	(zay);
	xiaotou	(shee-ow-toe)
thin	bao	(bow)
thing	dongxi	(doong-she);
	baihuo	(buy-hwaw)
thirsty	kele	(kuh-luh)
this	zhe	(juh);
	zhei	(jay)
those	na	(nah)
thousand-year egg	songhua dan	(soong-hwah dahn)
thread	xian	(shee-in)
throat	sangzi	(sahng-dzu)
thumb	muzhi	(muu-jr)
thumbtack	tu ding	(tuu deeng)
thunder (noun)	lei	(lay)
thunderstorm	leiyu	(lay-yuu)

Tian An Men (Gate of Heavenly Peace)	Tiananmen	(Tee-in-ahn-mun)
Tibet	Xizang	(She-zahng)
ticket	piao	(pee-ow)
ticket office	shoupiao chu	(show-pee-ow chuu)
ticket seller	maipiao-de	(my-pee-ow-duh)
tide	chao	(chow)
tie	lingdai	(leeng-die)
tiger	laohu	(lou-huu)
time	shijian shihou	(shr-jee-in); (shr-hoe)
timetable	shike biao	(shr-kuh bee-ow)
tin can	guantou	(gwahn-toe)
tip (gratuity)	xiaofei	(shee-ow-fay)
tired	leile	(lay-luh)
tissue paper	mianzhi	(mee-in-jr)
toast (bread)	kaomianbao	(kow-mee-in-bow)
together	yiqi	(ee-chee)
toilet	cesuo weishengjian	(tsuh-swaw); (way-shuung-jee-in)
toilet paper	shouzhi	(show-jr)
Tokyo	Dongjing	(Doong-jeeng)

tomatoes	xihongshi	(she-hoong-shr)
tomb	lingmu	(leeng-muu)
tomorrow	mingtian	(meeng-tee-in)
tongue	shetou	(shuh-toe)
tonight	jinwan	(jeen-wahn)
tool	gongju	(goong-juu)
tooth	ya	(yah)
toothache	yatong	(yah-toong)
toothbrush	yashua	(yah-shwah)
toothpaste	yagao	(yah-gow)
toothpick	yaqian	(yah-chee-in)
torch, flashlight	shoudiantong	(show-dee-in-toong)
tour	luxing	(luu-sheeng)
tour escort	lingdui	(leeng-dway)
tour group	luxingtuan	(luu-sheeng-twahn)
tourist	luke	(luu-kuh)
tournament	bisai	(bee-sigh)
toward	wang	(wahng)
towel	maojin	(mou-jeen)
tower	ta	(tah)
town	shizhen	(shr-jun)
toy	wanju	(wahn-juu)
toy store	wanju dian	(wahn-juu dee-in)

track (train)	tiegui	(tee-eh-gway)
trade, commerce	maoyi	(mou-ee)
trade fair	jiaoyi hui	(jee-ow-ee hway)
trademark	shang biao	(shahng bee-ow)
traffic	jiaotong	(jee-ow-toong)
traffic circle	jiaotong huandao	(jee-ow-toong hwahn-dow)
traffic light	hongludeng	(hoong-luu-duung)
train (dining car) (express train) (fast train) (reclining car) (sleeping car)	huoche can che te kuai kuai che tang yi wo pu	(hwaw-chuh); (tsahn chuh); (tuh kwie); (kwie chuh); (tahng yee); (waw puu)
train station	huoche zhan	(hwaw-chuh jahn)
tram, streetcar	dianche	(dee-in-chuh)
transaction	jiaoyi	(jee-ow-ee)
transfer (bank)	zhuanzhang	(jwahn-jahng)
transfer (train or bus line)	huan che	(hwahn chuh)
translate	fanyi	(fahn-ee)
translator	fanyi	(fahn-ee)
transportation	yunshu	(ywun-shuu)
transportation charges	yunshu feiyong	(ywun-shuu fay-yoong)
travel, trip	luxing	(luu-sheeng)

322

travel agency	luxing she	(luu-sheeng shuh)
traveler	luke	(luu-kuh)
traveler's check	luxing zhipiao	(luu-sheeng jr-pee-ow)
treatment (medical)	zhiliao	(jr-lee-ow)
tree	shu	(shuu)
trousers	kuzi	(ku-dzu)
truck	kache	(kah-chuh)
t-shirt	yuandongshan	(ywen-doong-shahn)
tuition	xuefei	(shu-eh-fay)
tumor	liu	(leo)
tunnel	suidao	(sway-dow)
turn, change direction	guaiwan	(gwie-wahn)
turn off (switch)	guandiao	(gwahn-dee-ow)
turn on (switch)	dakai	(dah-kigh)
turtle	haigui gu	(high-gway); (guu)
tutor	daoshi	(dow-shr)
tweezers	niezi	(nee-eh-dzu)
type, kind	lei yang	(lay); (yahng)
type, write	dazi	(dah-dzu)
typewriter	daziji	(dah-dzu-jee)

typhoon	taifeng	(tie-fuung)
typist	daziyuan	(dah-dzu-ywen)
typhus	banzhenshang-han	(bahn-jun-shahng-hahn)

U

ugly	nankan	(nahn-kahn)
ulcer	kuiyang	(kway-yahng)
umbrella	yusan	(yuu-sahn)
unacceptable	buxing	(buu-sheeng)
uncle	bofu	(bwo-fuu)
uncomfortable	bushufu buhaoshou	(buu-shuu-fuu); (buu-how-show)
underpass	dixia guodao	(dee-shee-ah gwaw-dow)
undershirt	neiyi	(nay-ee)
understand	dong	(doong)
underwear	neiyi	(nay-ee)
unemployed	shiye-de	(shr-yeh-duh)
uniform	zhifu	(jr-fuu)
unique	bieju	(bee-eh-juu)
unit, team	dui	(dway)

United Nations	Lianhe Guo	(Lee-in-huh Gwaw)
United States	Meiguo	(May-gwaw)
universal	pubian-de	(puu-bee-in-duh)
universe	yuzhou	(yuu-joe)
university	daxue	(dah-shu-eh)
up	shang	(shahng)
upstairs	loushang	(low-shahng)
urgent matter	jishi	(jee-shr)
urinate	xiaobian	(shee-ow-bee-in)
urine	niao	(nee-ow)

V

vacancy	kongfangjian	(koong-fahng-jee-in)
vacant	kong-de	(koong-duh)
vacation	fangjia	(fahng-jee-ah)
vaccination certificate	fangyi zheng	(fahng-ee juung)
vacuum flask	baowengping	(bow-wun-peeng)
valley	shangu	(shahng-guu)
valuable	zhengui	(jun-gway)

value	jiaqian	(jee-ah-chee-in)
vehicle	cheliang	(chuh-lee-ahng)
vegetable	shucai	(shuu-tsigh)
vegetarian	chisu-de	(chee-suu-duh)
venereal disease	xingbing	(sheeng-beeng)
vest	beixing	(bay-sheeng)
vicinity	fujin	(fuu-jeen)
video camera	luxiang ji	(luu-shee-ahng jee)
Vietnam	Yuenan	(Yu-eh-nahn)
view, scenery	fengjing	(fuung-jeeng)
village	cunzhuang	(tswun-jwahng)
vinegar	cu	(tsu)
visa	qianzheng	(chee-in-jung)
visit a person	baihui	(buy-hway)
visit a place	fangwen	(fahng-wun)
visitor, guest	keren	(kuh-wren)
visitor, tourist	youke	(yoe-kuh)
vocabulary	cihui	(tsu-hway)
vodka	futejia	(fuu-tuh-jee-ah)
voice	sheng	(shuung)
volleyball	paiqiu	(pie-cheo)
voltage	dianya	(dee-in-yah)
vomit	outu	(oh-tuu)
vote	toupiao	(toe-pee-ow)

wage, salary	gongzi	(goong-dzu)
wagon, cart	huoche	(hwaw-chuh)
waist	yao	(yow)
wait	deng	(duung)
waiter, waitress	fuwuyuan	(fuu-wuu-ywen)
waiting room	houke shi	(hoe-kuh shr)
wake up	xing	(sheeng)
walk (noun)	sanbu	(sahn-buu)
walk (verb)	zou	(zoe)
walking shoes	pingdi xie	(peeng-dee she-eh)
wall	qiang	(chee-ahng)
wallet	pijiazi qianbaor	(pee-jee-ah-dzu); (chee-in-bow-urr)
wall poster	qiangbao	(chee-ahng-bow)
want	yao	(yow)
war	zhanzheng	(jahn-jung)
warm	nuanhuo	(nwahn-hwaw)
wash, clean	xi	(she)
washable	kexi-de	(kuh-she-duh)
washbasin	xishouchi	(she-show-chee)
washing machine	xiyi ji	(she-ee jee)
wastebasket	zizhilou	(dzu-jr-low)

wastepaper	feizhi	(fay-jr)
watch (pocket) (wrist)	biao shoubiao	(bee-ow); (show-bee-ow)
water	shui	(shway)
waterfall	pubu	(puu-buu)
waterfront	haibin	(high-bin)
watermelon	xigua	(she-gwah)
waterproof	fangshui-de	(fahng-shway-duh)
water-ski	hua shui	(hwah shway)
wave (sea)	lang	(lahng)
way, lane	lu	(luu)
way out	chu lu	(chuu luu)
we	women	(waw-mun)
weak, feeble	ruo	(rwaw)
wealthy	youqian	(yoe-chee-in)
weather	tianqi	(tee-in-chee)
weather forecast	tianqi yubao	(tee-in-chee yuu-bow)
wedding	hunli	(hwun-lee)
week	xingqi	(sheeng-chee)
weekend	zhoumo	(joe-mwo)
weigh	cheng	(chuung)
weight	zhongliang	(joong-lee-ahng)
welcome	huanying	(hwahn-eeng)
well (good)	hao	(how)

well (water or oil)	jing	(jeeng)
west	xi	(she)
West	Xibianr	(She-bee-in-urr)
Western country	xiyang	(she-yahng)
Western food	xican	(she-tsahn)
Westernized	xihua-de	(she-hwah-duh)
Western medicine	xiyao	(she-yow)
Western toilet	zuoshi cesuo	(zwaw-shr tsuh-swaw)
wet	shi-de	(shr-duh)
wharf, jetty	matou	(mah-toe)
wheat	maizi	(my-dzu)
wheat flour	mian fen	(mee-in fin)
wholesale	pifa	(pee-fah)
wide, broad	kuan	(kwahn)
wife	qizi	(chee-dzu)
wild animal	ye shou	(yeh show)
wildlife	yeshengdongwu	(yeh-shuung-doong-wuu)
wind	feng	(fuung)
windbreaker	fengyi	(fuung-ee)
windmill	fengche	(fuung-chuh)
window	chuanghu	(chwahng-huu)
windy	guafeng-de	(gwah-fuung-duh)
wine	putaojiu	(puu-tou-jeo)

wineshop, pub	jiuba	(jeo-bah)
winter	dongtian	(doong-tee-in)
with	gen	(gun)
wok	chaocai guo	(chow-tsigh gwaw)
woman	nuren	(nuu-wren)
wood	mutou	(muu-toe)
wool	chunmao	(chwun-mou)
word	ci	(tsu)
work	gongzuo	(goong-zwaw)
worker	gongren	(goong-wren)
workshop	chejian	(chuh-jee-in)
world	shijie	(shr-jee-eh)
worship	chongbai	(choong-buy)
wound	dashang	(dah-shahng)
wrap	baozhuang	(bow-jwahng)
wrapping	pi	(pee)
wrist	shouwan	(show-wahn)
wristwatch	shou biao	(show bee-ow)
write	xie	(she-eh)
write down	ji	(jee)
writer	zuojia	(zwaw-jee-ah)
writing brush	mao bi	(mou bee)
writing paper	xinzhi	(sheen-jr)
written language	wen zi	(wun dzu)
wrong	cuo-le	(tswaw-luh)

X

xerox	fuyin	(fuu-een)
x-ray	x-guangpianzi	(x-gwahng-pee-in-dzu)

Y

Yangtse River	Chang Jiang	(Chahng Jee-ahng)
yard, courtyard	yuan zi	(ywen dzu)
yard (measure)	ma	(mah)
year	nian	(nee-in)
yearly	nian nian	(nee-in nee-in)
yellow	huangse	(hwahng-suh)
Yellow River	Huang He	(Hwahng Huh)
yesterday	zuotian	(zwaw-tee-in)
yogurt	suanniunai	(swahn-neo-nigh)
you (singular)	ni	(nee);
(plural)	nimen	(nee-mun)
young	nianqing	(nee-in-cheeng)
your	ni-de	(nee-duh)
youth	qiangnian	(chee-ahng-nee-in)

Z

zero	ling	(leeng)
zipper	lalian	(lah-lee-in)
zoo	dongwuyuan	(doong-wuu-ywen)

Other Books by Boye Lafayette De Mente

Japanese Etiquette and Ethics in Business
How to Do Business with the Japanese
Japanese Secrets of Graceful Living
Japan Encyclopedia
The Japanization of America
Nihon Ka Suru Amerika
Japan at Night—A Guide to Entertainment and Leisure in Japan
Discovering Cultural Japan
Japanese in Plain English
Korean Etiquette and Ethics in Business
Korean in Plain English
Chinese Etiquette and Ethics in Business
Business Guide to Japan
Japan Made Easy—All You Need to Know to Enjoy Japan
Etiquette Guide to Japan
Instant Japanese
Survival Japanese
Japanese for the Travel Industry
NTC's Dictionary of Japan's Cultural Code Words
NTC's Dictionary of China's Cultural Code Words